Wings of Our Own

Heroes, Happenings & History
of Air Force Spouses

Written and compiled by P.K. Johnson

Many thanks
for all you do!
P.K Johnson

Wingspan Publications

Library of Congress Catalog Card Number: 00-108007

ISBN 0-9701123-0-0

Cover design: Octavo Designs, Maryland
Interior design: The Printed Page, Phoenix, Arizona
Edited by Janice Murphy

Printed in the United States of America

Acknowledgments

My journey into the world of book writing began with a call from a college friend. Carolyn Stegman phoned, not only to discuss a book she was writing about women of achievement, but also to encourage me to write one about Air Force spouses. Her excitement was contagious. So, with her spirited urging, I decided to just dive in. The process took me on an incredible journey and I thoroughly enjoyed the ride.

The book's format changed several times as the project evolved. The criteria, however, always remained the same: each story was written *about* or *by* an Air Force spouse. I am grateful for the support of so many people, especially my husband Si, whose positive attitude and enthusiasm kept me focused. Our thirty-three year military adventure has given us many treasured memories and provided the foundation for this endeavor. Our children, Jennifer and Tyler, were raised in the military, and are emotionally connected to the stories in this book. They, along with our daughter-in-law Shelley, were eager to see them recorded. My mother, Helen Kamykowski, who is also an author, offered me inspiration; and my mother-in-law, Lou Johnson, a Navy spouse, heartily endorsed my intentions.

Through friends, word of mouth and the Internet, I was able to reach many who had stories to share. Every story I received fortified my commitment to this undertaking. I am extremely grateful to Dede Ralston, Cynthia Hornburg, Karen Pfeiffer, Jane LeMay Lodge, Janice Missildine, Karen Spiker and my friends at McGuire AFB for their help and guidance.

The journey would not have been as meaningful and successful without them.

In addition to those whose stories are a part of this book, many others have provided valuable insight and assistance to me. Among them are: Suellen Lansell, Pat Thomas, Sandy Troeber, Lisa Reichard, Duane Reed, Jack Barbeau and Air Force Village, Bonnie Carroll, Murray Green, Shirley Watts and the Enlisted Men's Widows and Dependants Home, Tony Burshnick, Marlene Hawley, Jim Reagan, Ron Rand, Diane Chikaris, the Public Affairs Office in the Pentagon, Brenda Applegate, Chris Wasdin, Vicki Thomas, and Praushad Abdul Rasheed.

Wings is unique because it highlights the role of the military spouse rather than focusing on the life of the service member. Volumes of books have been written about military greats. Less than a handful have been written about the contribution and sacrifices of the their spouses.

P.K. Johnson

foreword

It was an honor when my friend P. K. Johnson asked me to write the foreword to her wonderful collection of stories about military spouses. P. K. herself is an inspiring woman, a tireless dynamo who wanted to chronicle AF history from the perspective of the spouse. Perhaps she asked me to write this because of my unique background. I grew up in the military. My father served 39 years as a pilot in the Air Force. I am married to an AF pilot now…out of the cockpit and flying a desk as they say. I have seen the military from all sides, including through the eyes of the civilian community during my first marriage. That twenty-three year hiatus made me appreciate the military even more. I love this life. I loved it then—I relish it now. P. K's book encourages us to reflect on what we bring to this community and what draws us to this way of life. She wants us to take a closer look at what it is that keeps us moving forward in times that are often fraught with adversities. Military life IS a serious existence, and it is full of sacrifices, as each of us is aware daily.

Military life is also changing—change is good. Change is unsettling. What is the constant that keeps us energized, happy? What gives us a sense of history, a can do spirit, a love of country? I was touched by every story in this book. The military has provided all of us with a close knit, spirited community. But who are the people responsible for this comfort and security? We have a sense of togetherness that nurtures our lives and brings us peace in times of stress. It's all about people…and P.K. gives us their stories.

What's mine? Well, it's day zero, or day one, however you choose to look at it. It's moving day! As we said growing up in an AF family—"we are off on another one of life's great adventures!"

As I write I'm moving to another country to live. I'm ready to grow and change. This nomadic life is in my blood. I love it! Why? I get "high" on the opportunity to broaden my horizons, a chance to learn and see new things. I can reinvent myself. Hopefully, I'll become even more selfreliant. I've been as organized as I can be—now I just have to have faith in myself, my marriage, and my family that we will take our security with us and bloom where we are planted. It's the ultimate test of teamwork. A challenge, a willingness to be flexible. These gifts are being handed to me. I'm ready, I want to take advantage and I am eager to embrace a different life style. I want to hit the ground running and make a difference in my new setting.

What will be my goals this time? Volunteering? Helping to make the road less bumpy for others? Helping others see the importance of their contributions? Praise for a job well done? Soothing another's pain? Being there for a friend in need? Projecting a positive image of our country to foreign nations? Learn to play tennis? Learn a new language? Anyway, I'm excited about life. How many in this world can say they have been given this gift of change time and time again?

The people you will meet in this heartwarming and often moving account are teachers, authors, caretakers, volunteers, daredevils, and friends of the world they inhabit. Their service and dedication have enriched the lives of those around them. They have looked beyond themselves and have made the military community a better place. Ms. Johnson chronicles their individual journeys with love and skill. In presenting the lives of these airmen's wives and husbands, P. K. makes her own invaluable contribution to military history. It is a book that will be enjoyed by everyone in the military and by all those who wish to know a little more about the families of the men and women who serve our country with pride. These stories are awesome!

Dede Ralston

Wings of Our Own

Contents

Wings of Our Own

Introduction

Wings of Our Own brings alive the role of the Air Force spouse. This collection of personal narratives and anecdotes documents the history and contributions of U.S. Air Force spouses, past and present. It honors those military mates "who also serve" and have inspired or touched us with their true tales of military life. It is their shared experiences that make this book possible. They provide a linkage to the past and inspiration for the future.

Some stories are emotionally charged, some are humorous, others are educational and inspiring. All are heartwarming and all demonstrate the bonds and similarities that connect us.

My hope is that every military spouse who reads this book will be filled with pride about who we are, applaud the accomplishments of those before us as well as our peers, and enjoy the special bond we share. I also hope to acquaint those who are not a part of the armed services with this unique lifestyle and the contributions of the military spouse.

Enjoy!

Paulette K. Johnson

Friendship

"Some people come into our lives and quietly go; others stay for a while and leave footprints on our hearts and we are never the same."

Author Unknown

Wings of Our Own

Friendship

I believe in women. I believe in their innate goodness and in their ability to give. I believe in the way they can look past themselves and see the need in other people. I am happy to be one, and to enjoy the company of so many good ones.

When I married my handsome young lieutenant, I was sure that this man, who had pursued me so hotly, would entertain me for the rest of my life. I thought he was all that I needed. I built my nest, ready for a life of romance and adventure with my man in blue.

Well, the ink was barely dry on the marriage license when he dropped me 3,000 miles from home, and with barely a blink of the eye, (and not a bit of shame) picked up the Air Force as his "mistress." How could I compete with that sleek silver bird?—She took him to dizzying heights—he "touched the face of God" with her! She took him to places around the world that I had only dreamed of—places I didn't know existed, and she paid for the trip!

No amount of crying or complaining would make him leave "her." I quickly discovered that my road to happiness would have to be partially paved by me. The fun, sexy guy I had married was only around a few days at a clip. That is when I discovered the OWC, and the company of women.

As women married to military men, we find that we can almost never depend on our husbands to "be there." They leave us to eat macaroni and cheese with crying babies while they are eating at Sushi Bars in Japan, seeing castles in Germany and wiping sand out of their eyes in the desert.

They leave us with broken dishwashers, kids with broken arms, and frankly, sometimes broken hearts from broken promises. This is not so with women friends. We help each other mop up the water from the floor, get the kids to the emergency room, and wipe away each other's tears. And we NEVER call each other when HIS car is in the driveway!!

I have come to believe that "the mission" will always get done by our boys in blue. Commanders had often told wives that the mission couldn't be done without us-but I'm convinced that it was often accomplished over us, under us, around us and even through us. I couldn't have made it as an Air Force wife without my fellow wives beside me.

My life is forever touched by the women whom I have been blessed to call friends. It is so much larger than had I stayed and lived in my hometown. I have learned to give, as well as receive, acts of love and selflessness in both my marriage and my friendships. My life has been rich and happy as an Air Force wife.

My husband of 24 years still pursues me hotly and does his best to entertain me when he is home. He recognizes the sacrifices I have made that have enabled him to "slip the surly bonds." And blesses the women who have kept me company and kept me sane.

Yes, my life has been rich and happy as an Air Force wife, but it has been richer from being an Air Force friend. Here's to the OWC and what it has done for women like me.

Eileen Losi

The Support Team

At my high school reunion last year, one of the guys I had struggled through Physics lab with asked me, "And what do you do?"

On this occasion, I had already approached that query from several different angles. After being surrounded all evening by teachers, stewardesses, nurses and even a Ph.D., it was getting to be a fairly intimidating question. Then, in a flash of inspiration, I came up with the definitive answer.

"I'm the support team," I stated proudly.

It wasn't until I thought about those words later on that I realized how true they are. We as Air Force wives, not only support our husbands—keeping the home fires burning, while acting as single parents much of the time, and sleeping cuddled next to empty pillows with the doors duly bolted against intruders, and yet, being able to greet them with a warm smile and a hug when they return—we support each other.

We support each other every day in little ways. Like watching your neighbor's kids for a few hours to preserve her sanity. Like listening sympathetically to the lonely newlywed whose husband is stuck out in the system for an extra week. Like making that special effort to reach out and involve the shy newcomer. A soft-spoken friend of mine pointed out to me that it's almost impossible to be a member of the Air Force family and remain introverted (a fact that would otherwise have completely escaped my rather aggressive attention).

Although we know each other sometimes only fleetingly, the friendships we make among Air Force wives seem more intimate and lasting than others. Why? It goes even deeper than shared experiences, to the security of knowing that when you need a friend, or a surrogate mother, or just someone who cares, you've got a whole team of people you can lean on. And they can depend on you.

Lynn Perry
McGuire OWC *Flair*
November 1982

A Toast to Good Friends

Friday afternoons would roll around, and I'd wander out on the front porch. Housework was done, kids were off playing, and supper was in the oven.

One of my friends was likely to be in view: Kathy pulling weeds, Barbara walking the dog, or Gail on the way over to borrow a cup of broccoli.

More often than not, one of us would call out, "There's a semi-truck broken down on the Beltway, and the guys won't be home 'til after 8. Come over and have a glass of wine."

I especially treasured the Friday afternoons we drank our wine (or diet soda if we were feeling fat) on Kathy's patio. We always laughed and talked of many subjects.

Stories of Kathy's husband's dead maiden aunt often slipped into our conversation. Then, one twilight evening, Aunt Kay walked in and sat down with us in the form of lovely, crystal wine goblets.

We admired the shining goblets into which Kathy was pouring wine. What a contrast they made to the large green jug!

Unaware of what we were holding above the unforgiving cement of the patio, we blanched when Kathy told us the goblets were her legacy from Aunt Kay and were worth $50 each. Kathy was of the opinion that things were meant to be used and enjoyed. That was why she had inherited the goblets—Aunt Kay was of the same mind.

Friday nights were special, and on Kathy's patio, with cheap wine in Aunt Kay's delicately patterned goblets, we passed the time in a special camaraderie.

Then it happened. The bubble burst. Brigadoon disappeared into the mists. Camelot crumbled. The Pentagon pouted. We got orders.

I put on a brave face. I said, "It's lovely there. The house is new. We'll learn to sail. We'll like it as we've liked it everywhere we've lived." But I didn't want to go. I'd never been as content anywhere as in that 20-year-old house that needed a new roof and sat next door to not just one, but *three* good friends. Kathy brought me a going-away gift. The card read, "We all take a little something from everyone we meet. Some things are more visible than others. I couldn't think of a better 'I'll miss you and housewarming' gift. You have been a treasured friend and neighbor. Love and Cheers!"

I opened the beautifully wrapped box with the happy anticipation that accompanies an unexpected gift. The tissue paper unfolded to reveal a gift that stabbed me in the heart— one of Aunt Kay's goblets.

It has taken a year for the grief to ease. For that long, I could not bear to pour wine into Aunt Kay's goblet. I would reach for it and then draw back my hand as from a hot stove. But last night, I poured wine into it and drank with dry eyes and fond memories of Kathy, Barbara, and Gail.

Soon I'll pour wine into the goblet and offer it to Mary Jo, Katie, or Cathie. Dear new friends are here. They deserve to drink from Aunt Kay's goblet—for they enabled me to drink from it.

Lois Hansen
Reprinted with permission of Army Times

Friendship Chain

An endless chain of hellos and good-byes
join together the diverse lives
of women like us,
who pledge our hearts to
men who choose the warrior's path.

Some links are iron,
forged in understanding born of shared joys and fears,
tempered by accepted differences,
softly burnished by years
of losing and finding one another again.

Others are more tentative stuff,
a curious alloy of reassurance and warmth
not bearing the whole weight of our hearts perhaps,
but spanning the spaces between those who do,
the empty places where change and duty leave us adrift.

Perhaps one measure of our lives thus far
is counted in the pattern of links we leave joined
to other women like us.
Perhaps in the intricate lacing of friendship's web
Lies the best of who we are.

Maryellen Mills
July 1999

Portable Palettes — Lasting Friendship

Air Force wives soon learn to be proficient in packing up and moving on. But the happiest are those who nurture family, friends and their own talents, even as they call a new place home.

Over twenty years ago a special friendship was born at Scott Air Force Base in Illinois. Margaret Hoybach, Carla O'Connor, Nancy Rankin and Marilyn Jacobs, all wives of young Air Force officers, shared an interest in painting. During the three years they spent together, living in the nation's heartland, they worked on new techniques, sharing ideas with one another, and their talents with their husbands' organizations, the Officers' Wives' Club and the community in general.

When O'Connor's husband was reassigned to Holland, the women made a pact. Hoybach says, "We would meet somewhere once a year to paint, no matter where each of us was." They have kept that pact. Even though their husbands are long retired from the Air Force, a real bond will always exist.

While together at Scott, they had begun the practice of taking an annual "sabbatical" together, going off from family to paint and hone their professional skills. After over twenty years they remain faithful to the group get-together. "If you don't come, you practically have to have a note from your doctor that you've passed away," says Hoybach, whose first "studio" in Travis Air Force Base housing was an expanded playpen she worked in to keep her three toddlers from getting into the paints.

The longest Rankin and her husband were in any one place was two or three years, but it was usually more like a year or 18 months. When Lt. Colonel Jim finally retired, they settled down in the Northwest where Carla and Lt. Colonel Mike were already ensconced. The two wives decided to open a gallery together.

The first building they rented had no heat, no bathroom, a leaky roof, an outside door that refused to close and, on first sight, a crop of huge mushrooms growing in one corner of the floor. But these wives were used to "making do."

"When you can walk in and say, 'Well, this isn't so bad. A little paper, and I can fix it up,' you know this has to come from having made 14 or 15 military moves," O'Connor says.

"We've even developed a different palette for each place we've lived," Rankin adds. "When I was in Oklahoma, it was very earth-toned." Jacobs, who now lives on acres of virgin forest in Washington's Cascade mountains, agrees, noting the green and white that show up in her watercolors now.

Like so many other Air Force wives, they treasure the gift of the sisterhood their nomadic lives bestowed upon them. Despite the fact they are each award-winning artists of considerable renown now, they continue their lifelong pattern of "giving back," both to their communities, as well as one another.

"We've shored each other up through all of our ups and downs over the years," Hoybach says. "It was very hard when you had to move an art career, because you don't bring your following with you each time." What they did take along—and never lost—is a bond of friendship so special that neither change of place nor the passage of time will sever it.

© *Joan Brown*

Picasso Never Had to Drive in a Carpool

Not only is Maggie Hoybach an accomplished and award winning artist, lecturer and teacher, she is also an entertainer. On the lecture circuit she has often been referred to as "Erma Bombeck with a paintbrush." Her presentation "Picasso Never Had to Drive in a Carpool," is filled with stories about being an artist in the real world of children, pets and carpools.

Recently she has added an educational television series to her colorful resumé. In 1998 she began filming "The Artistry of Margaret Hoybach" for public television in Fairfax, Virginia. The multi-talented Hoybach, in tandem with her vibrant personality, continues to inspire and motivate others. She says, "I love what I do and I love to share it. It's my way of giving back."

Paulette K. Johnson

"Spouses' Dining-In" Speech

Below are some excerpts from a speech I gave at the 3rd Annual Spouses' Combat Dining-In. The Tinker AWACS spouses enthusiastically sponsored this event. I attended the 1st all-spouse Dining-In and was excited to return for a "reunion" to be their guest speaker. This was always a spirited occasion complete with combat dress, toasts to "official" spouses, a President of the Mess and a Ms. Vice.

My speech describes the Air Force spouse using each letter in AF SPOUSE.

A in AF SPOUSE is for ATTITUDE.

You as an AF spouse look at life as your "cup being half-full, not half-empty." For example, moving is a challenge, not a disaster; separation is a time for self-reflection, not isolation; and living in foreign lands and remote places is an adventure. Your motto would be "Conserve energy and concentrate only on the positive. Nothing lasts forever, even the current assignment."

The F in AF SPOUSE stands for FLEXIBILITY.

I am sure you have heard the saying "flexibility is the key to success." Nowhere is that more important than in the home of the AF family.

    You have to constantly adjust to new surroundings and schedules.

- You have to find new baby-sitters, dentists, doctors, churches and schools. In some cases this all has to be done in a foreign country.

- You have to be creative and decorate around white walls and various shades of brown tile. And all on a budget!

The first S in AF SPOUSE stands for SUPPORTIVE.

This may be the third letter of the group, but it is your number one attribute. Being supportive includes making sacrifices—even when you don't feel like it. And many of these sacrifices are SILENT SACRIFICES—no fanfare, no recognition, no medals, no words on an APR or OER. Nor do you want any. You have spent many nights alone taking care of a sick child and celebrated Christmas and/or Thanksgiving alone.

There have been many missed recitals, graduations, anniversaries, soccer games, and birthday parties. All through this you support your spouse's choice to serve his country, wherever that may be.

The P in AF SPOUSE is for POSITIVE THINKERS.

You, as a military spouse, could easily be the model for the very popular book, *Simple Abundance Journal of Gratitude*, by Sarah Ban Breathnach.

If you haven't read her book let me very briefly explain its premise…It is easy to be grateful and happy when life is going well and the way we think it should. But when things get tough, it is hard to remain positive. In her workbook, Ms. Breathnach suggests you list five things a day for which you are grateful. If you do this everyday as she suggests, you will, after a couple of months, begin to look at life differently.

It is a simple philosophy, but one Air Force spouses adopted years ago. You did it long before it was mentioned on the *Oprah Show*.

O stands for OPEN TO NEW CHALLENGES.

As spouses you take advantage of the opportunities that open up when you move from station to station. You embrace change and make it work for you. Some examples are: changing career fields, starting a family, becoming a full-time parent, getting a degree or some specialized training, volunteering, or writing a book like I did.

U is for UNIQUENESS.

Did anyone ever ask you what you do as an Air Force wife? Hard to explain, isn't it? Although it can be fun and adventuresome, a good portion of energy is spent dealing with the challenges we all face.

I'm sure many of you are familiar with the following description of a military wife. It stresses the UNIQUE-NESS of the military spouse.

The Military Wife

The good Lord was creating a model for military wives and was into his sixth day of overtime when an angel appeared. She said, "Lord you seem to be having a lot of trouble with this one. What's wrong with the standard model?"

The Lord replied, "Have you seen the specs on this order? She has to be completely independent, possess the qualities of both mother and father, be a perfect hostess to four or forty with an hour's notice, run on black coffee, handle every emergency imaginable without a manual, be able to carry on cheerfully, even if she is pregnant and has the flu, and she must be willing to move to a new location 10 times in 17 years. And oh, yes, she must have six pairs of hands." The angel shook her head. "Six pairs of hands? No way."

The Lord continued, "Don't worry, we will make other military wives to help her. And we will give her an unusually strong heart so it can swell with pride in her husband's achievements, sustain the pain of separations, beat soundly when it is overworked and tired, and be large enough to say—'I understand'—when she doesn't, and say —'I love you,' regardless."

"Lord," said the angel, touching his arm gently, "Go to bed and get some rest. You can finish this tomorrow."

"I can't stop now," said the Lord. "I am so close to creating something UNIQUE. Already this model heals herself when she is sick, can put up six unexpected guests for the weekend, wave goodbye from a pier, a runway, or a depot, and understand why it is important that he leaves."

The angel circled the model of the military wife, looked at it closely and sighed, "It looks fine, but it is too soft."

"She might look soft," replied the Lord, "but she has the strength of a lion. You would not believe what she can endure."

Finally, the angel bent over and ran her finger across the cheek of the Lord's creation. "There's a leak," she announced. "Something is wrong with the construction. I am not surprised that it is cracked. You are trying to put too much into this model."

The Lord appeared offended at the angel's lack of confidence. "What you see is not a leak," he said. "It is a tear."

"A tear? What is it there for?" asked the angel.

The Lord replied, "It is there for joy, sadness, pain, disappointment, loneliness, pride and dedication to all the values that she and her husband hold dear."

"You are a genius!" exclaimed the angel.

The Lord looked puzzled and replied, "I didn't put it there."

Author Unknown

The second S in AF SPOUSE is for SELFLESSNESS.

You are always giving to others. Many of you spend countless hours doing volunteer work. We have spouses helping each other and people in our AF and civilian community, working with schools and hospitals and much, much more. You MAKE A DIFFERENCE! All this good work has a wonderful spiral effect. It is contagious.

Last but not least. E is for ENTHUSIASTIC.

It has been my pleasure to work with many enthusiastic spouses. A good example is the group that organized tonight's gathering. You have shown your enthusiasm by planning this Spouses' Combat Dining-In. In fact, enthusiasm is an understatement!

When Air Force Secretary Dr. Sheila Widnall was visiting Tinker AFB she told a little story about enthusiasm and attitude that I would like to share with you. It was about a shoe manufacturer who was contemplating marketing shoes in a Third World country. He sent two people down to research the market. The first person reported to the boss that there was NO market there because "no one wore shoes." The second person reported that there was a BIG market there because "no one wore shoes!"

Thanks for always being like that enthusiastic person in the story and for sharing your enthusiasm and wonderful attitude with others.

I've listed only a few of the words used to describe the AF spouse. She is so much more. Let's stand and toast the AF spouse.

Paulette K. Johnson

Who's Cookin' Tonight?

What do you do when you decide you spend "way too much time in the kitchen"? You start a cooking co-op, of course. That's what spouses Angie Spencer, Olivia Rabinowitch, Bridget Kingsford and Gina Haefele did.

The idea first surfaced when they were all together one New Year's Eve. That night the discussion centered on what they could do to improve their lifestyles. Angie mentioned she had read an interesting article in the newspaper about a cooking co-op. With that idea in mind, they decided to pool their resources and organize a meal exchange.

Each member cooks only one night during the workweek, but cooks enough for the eighteen people involved in the co-op. At first they began with only the entrée, and gradually, after six months of trial and error, they managed the whole meal. It was particularly helpful when their husbands were deployed to Kosovo. Gina recalls, "We all ate together frequently. It was a good time to let the kids play and allowed us moms some adult conversation."

Co-op families usually cook on the same night every week and deliver a hot meal to each of the other members. They are on their own for the weekend. "It has proven to be a great time saver and allows us much more freedom now that we're not cooking every night," Gina explains. They get together every eight weeks to plan menus. Each participant decides what meals to cook. The bottom line is to keep it simple.

Not having to cook every night isn't the only benefit of co-op dining. Gina points out, "We eat healthier meals, don't eat fast food as often, and the children are experiencing a variety of different foods." In addition, they find they are spending less at the commissary. Meal planning and cooking for 16-18 people allows them to buy in bulk, take advantage of any sales, and use coupons.

What do you do when you want to share this idea with other families? You write a book, of course, and that's what these four spouses did. *Who's Cookin' Tonight* provides a step-by-step guide on how to start a co-op, ensure food safety and features over 100 of their favorite recipes. The foursome has also discussed their book and co-op on a local TV talk show.

Increasing their free time by getting out of the kitchen has always been one of their goals. The friendships they have forged have been an added bonus. Gina says, "We've all grown very close since our co-op started and it will be hard to leave it when we PCS."

Paulette K. Johnson

History

"*I am only one; but still I am one. I cannot do everything, but still I can do something; I will not refuse to do the something I can do.*"

Helen Keller

Family "Matters"

The impact of Eleanor "Bee" Arnold's contributions to the Air Force can still be felt today. She lived in tumultuous times. A World War was being fought. Drastic changes in lifestyle affected nearly every American household. Servicemen and women and their families were facing extended separations and uncertainty.

The Army Air Corp had become the Army Air Forces to coordinate status with the other branches of the Army. Bee's husband, General Henry "Hap" Arnold was the commander of the AAF. At his urging, Bee encouraged all wives to put their social activities aside and contribute to the war effort by doing volunteer work. Bee set the example and immersed herself in volunteer activities. It required courage, skill and stamina.

For several years during World War II she worked seven days a week. Her husband gave her an office and an aide to help organize her efforts. She recalled in an interview with Colonel Murray Green, "…I'd work at night, too, because I would be called up about some girl who arrived in town and had no place to sleep. Well, those were busy days."

War, family separations, waiting wives, and volunteerism set the stage for Bee Arnold's contributions. Her pursuit to make things better for military families became the cornerstone of many programs in the Air Force today. Some are listed as follows.

Air Force Family

This very popular theme would become a benchmark in Air Force life. It is Bee Arnold who is credited with creating the term "Air Force Family." She was a devoted mother of five children. Both she and General Arnold were well aware of the value and importance of family—they lost a son while stationed in San Diego.

Air Force Aid Society

Mrs. Arnold led the way for the creation of the Air Force Aid Society. General Arnold told his wife, "We have got to have some sort of organization to take care of the wives of these fliers." He added, "I want you to go to Washington tomorrow, and get this thing started."[1]

It didn't take her long. Several officers and spouses got together, created a charter, and established the Air Force Aid Society. The charter was granted with one condition—the organization was not allowed to solicit funds; they could only accept donations. The Army Emergency Relief gave them $600,000 to begin operations. It was an immediate success, and because of its popularity, did not need to solicit funds. The donations poured in. By the end of the war they had accumulated nine million dollars. Someone donated a valuable letter from Abraham Lincoln to sell to generate funds.[2]

---

1   Colonel Murray Green, Interview with Mrs. Bee Arnold, March 11, 1970.
2   Ibid.

National Association of Air Forces Women

This group organized wives for volunteer work in support of the war effort. The "silver wings," with the initials NAAFW proudly etched in the center, identified each member. At one point this group printed a monthly newsletter to help increase the flow of information to the wives. Ruth Spaatz, wife of Assistant Chief General Carl "Tooey" Spaatz, kept the group organized.

"Spotter" System

During wartime, wives were integrated with their new environment through the "spotter" system designed by Bee Arnold. It was used "to spot wives and help them find their spot." "Spotter" was a popular term used when searching for aircraft. Mrs. Arnold sent each spouse a welcome letter along with an information page to be completed by the spouse. This connection helped wives and families feel more secure in their new environment. Many spouses' organizations continued the spotter tradition until the 1980s.

OWC Charter Revision

It was also Bee who encouraged the wives' clubs to have an elected board rather than management by the commander's spouse. Initially, Mrs. Arnold suggested this so that she would be free to participate in more volunteer activities.

The Army Air Forces was fortunate to have had the leadership of General and Mrs. Arnold. General Arnold guided the AAF through a World War. Mrs. Arnold guided their most precious commodity—their families. Bee, although petite in stature, left behind a very large legacy.

Domestic Scene at Fort Myer—Circa 1943

General Hap Arnold invited two distinguished wartime journalists, Corey Ford and Alastair MacBain, to his home for dinner. Dinner was late that night in Quarters 8 at Fort Myer, because the General did not get home from his Pentagon office until well after 8:00 p.m. The nerves were a bit frayed and the famous smile was wan. When the entrée was served, the general complained to Mrs. Arnold that he was getting tired of chicken and wished he could have beef. Mrs. Arnold looked at her visitors, sadly, and said, "Hap doesn't know there's a war on."

Colonel Murray Green, USAF Ret.
Air Force Magazine
April 1972

Air Force Officers' Wives' Clubs

Martha Washington was a military spouse. In the book *Campfollowing: A History of the Military Wife,* Betty Alt and Bonnie Stone describe Martha Washington's role as a military spouse. "With the aid of the other officers' wives, both at home and in the camps, she formed what may have been the forerunner of the Officers' Wives' Club (OWC) and the Family Services program. While these social gatherings provided a sense of camaraderie for the war-weary wives, they also were designed to help the war effort. Circles of women knitted and sewed for the troops, rolled bandages from cast-off linen, and helped care for the ill and wounded."

Below is a timeline depicting the history of the Air Force Officers' Wives' Clubs.

1923 The Air Service branch of the Army was formed under the leadership of General Mason Patrick. On May 16, 1923, his wife Grace Patrick gathers over forty wives together in her home. They organized

> Mrs. Patrick, a great lady of the old school, obviously had initiative and imagination as well as compassion. It was she who first brought a pattern of unity into the lives of the flyers' wives. Perhaps she recognized the need of pride and esprit among the wives of those pioneer flyers. Perhaps she knew also how close death's wings hovered over those fragile "crates." Undoubtedly she was aware that friendship and family feeling eased worries and tension and fears.
>
> Ethel Kuter, "We Care" 1985

the Air Service Ladies' Club. The club established membership, hospital and entertainment committees.

1923-1947 Meetings and social gatherings were held regularly. Minutes of the Air Service Ladies' Club meetings were kept in a little black book. These minutes were filed in 1953 with the Air Force Historical Foundation. When World War II began the wives' clubs' activities were suspended so the women could support the war effort through volunteerism. Most volunteer activities were directed toward the American Red Cross.

> When World War II kicked in, Mildred Stearley and her husband, Ralph were stationed in Washington, D.C. Mildred got involved in the Army emergency relief activities through the woman's club. This involved taking care of any problems families had after their husbands received orders. "I had an interesting experience one day," she begins. "I went down and was sitting at my desk looking at some papers. I saw a notebook in there and I opened it and, lo and behold, it was the secretary's minutes of the first Air Force Woman's Club. Mother was one of the charter members. I saw her signature down there on that first meeting. I got such a kick out of that."
>
> Sandra Troeber
> Interview with Mrs. Mildred Stearley
> Air Force Village

After World War II when the Air Force became a separate service, the wives' clubs began to flourish. They became known as the Officers' Wives' Club. Their role expanded to the community and more emphasis was put on raising money for charity. Thrift Shops were organized. Most wives did not work outside the home. Childcare was a problem so the Wives' Clubs created and staffed the first base childcare centers.

Hats, gloves, calling cards and New Year's Day receptions were a part of this era. In 1953 an "Orientation Course for the Wives of Potential Commanders" was designed and presented at Maxwell AFB.[3]

1960s The war in Vietnam brought an increase in all service personnel. According to Carol Keller in her book, *The Air Force Wife Handbook*, "Most women became 'waiting wives' in informal groups and groups sponsored by Family Services and wives' clubs; they bonded together and they grieved together." Many wives went to live with their families. Some joined their husbands, unofficially. There was tension at home and abroad created by the unpopularity of the war.

Nineteen welcoming coffees were given for over 2,000 new members. Hours of planning and preparation went into the wonderful programs for the year. Approximately 1,600 members were entertained at the luncheons, between 200 and 300 at each of the teas.

Maxwell OWC State of the Union Message
Mrs. Lawrence M. Watson, President
June 1962

3   Mrs. Ethel Kuter, wife of General Lawrence Kuter planned and initiated the course. In 1954, nine hundred were invited to attend.

During the 60s the Officers' Wives' Clubs committed their efforts to the establishment of the Air Force Village. Plans for the Air Force Enlisted Men's Widows and Dependents Home Foundation were initiated and supported by the Enlisted Wives' Clubs.

1970s   This decade enjoyed more married than single members in the service. OWC membership doubled. One club, the Maxwell Officers' Wives' Club remained close to 1300 members throughout the 70s. Most OWC activities were daytime functions, such as Coffees and Luncheons. Reservations were necessary at some clubs' coffees because attendance was so large. Etiquette rules began to relax—no more hats or gloves.

At the same time, women began to question their role both in society as well as at home. Following their civilian counterparts, women began entering the job market in increasing numbers.

1980s   This decade saw restructuring for the wives' clubs as membership began to decline. OWC activities were streamlined. More evening functions were introduced. Some clubs changed their name to Officers' Spouses' Club to include male spouses and be more "politically correct." The concept of "choice" in society found its way into Air Force family life. The Blue Ribbon Panel[4] was formed and was a catalyst in shaping the role of the Air Force spouse. The

---

4   Refer to article in this book entitled "The Blue Ribbon Panel" on page 47.

Family Support Centers became involved with the needs of the family.

1990s   Drawdown, base closures, generation "X" characterize this decade. As Lydia Sloan Cline states in her book *Today's Military Wife, 3rd Edition,* "We are no longer expected to devote ourselves exclusively to promoting our husbands' careers. Today it is common for a wife to have her own career, and many military families cope with the same phenomena that have swept the rest of the country—the two-income family and the latchkey child."

This decade's OWCs are very small compared to the 70s and 80s. Childcare for stay-at-home mothers, as in past decades, continues to be a problem. Long hours, frequent deployments and the lure of high paying jobs in the civilian sector contribute to the retention problem.

Arlington Ladies

Sympathetic but upbeat.
Ceremonial but caring.
Respectful but warm.
Proud but unassuming.

These words describe the Air Force Arlington Ladies who, despite heat, rain, wind, snow or ice attend the funeral of every member of the Air Force—active, retired or veteran.

This special group celebrated their 50th anniversary in 1998. It all began with Gladys Vandenberg, wife of General Hoyt S. Vandenberg. As chief of staff of the Air Force, General Vandenberg and his wife lived close to Arlington cemetery. Gladys would often walk the hallowed grounds. Both attended funerals there.

They noticed that some of the airmen laid to rest in the cemetery had no one present at the graveside besides the chaplain and the honor guard. They discussed how sad it was that these airmen, who had served so bravely and so proudly, were often sent to their "final posting" alone. Mrs. Vandenberg was so moved she came up with a way to show that the Air Force family did indeed care.

At first Gladys Vandenberg attended every Air Force funeral at Arlington herself. She talked with others about her commitment. It didn't take long before her enthusiasm and dedication to these efforts caught on. Soon after, the Air Force Officers' Wives' Club of Washington decided to form a committee to serve along with Mrs. Vandenberg. Once organized, finding volunteers for this worthwhile and rewarding service was not difficult. Eventually the other services followed suit; the Army in 1973 and the Navy in 1985. Together they all share a small office in the cemetery's administration building.

Each volunteer typically serves one day a month. On any given day there may be from one to five burials. Services can begin as early as 8:30 a.m. and end as late as 4:00 p.m. Weather conditions are almost never a factor and never a deterrent for them. They come prepared for the elements, yet dressed properly to show respect. A military escort is by the volunteer's side. Volunteers don't wear black since they do not see themselves as mourners. They are with those who are celebrating the military life of the deceased. After the flag is formally handed over to the family, an Arlington Lady presents them with a sympathy card, signed by the Air Force chief of staff and his wife on behalf of the men and women of the Air Force. A personal note of condolence from the Arlington Lady is also given to the family. This interaction can be both emotionally exhausting and rewarding at the same time.

Because of their schedule, not much time is spent interacting with other Air Force spouses on the committee. In order to share their stories of gratitude, and build camaraderie, they organize several social gatherings—including a Christmas Holiday Party for the Air Force Honor Guard and Ceremonial Brass, who perform duties at Arlington National Cemetery. A quarterly newsletter keeps volunteers up to date.

The reasons are simple and varied as to why each volunteers. A past chairman, Suellen Lansell, says she finds it "a very satisfying and unique way to serve the Air Force family. I feel a part of Air Force history." Many on the committee have served faithfully for years—one has served thirty-five years. And yes, men have served on the committee too! Indeed, with an average of six hundred burials a year, the volunteers over the past fifty years have touched the lives of many Air Force families.

General Vandenberg would have been proud to know that on the day of his funeral in Arlington, not just one, but almost all of the Arlington Ladies were present to say goodbye to him.[5]

Paulette K. Johnson
Source: Suellen Lansell

Ramonde Thompson reminisces about her interest in volunteering as an Arlington Lady fifty years ago. "I only went to one funeral with two other new volunteers to watch what we were to do when on our own. I was thirty years old, the other two women were in their forties. It broke me up and it was plain to see I'd never do in that job. Mrs V. was very kind and said 'When you are older, you'll understand.' Now I do."

September 13, 1998

---

5 Metcalf, Jane, *Dowry of Uncommon Women*, p.213.

Air Force Village

> *"Make no mistake about it. Retirement facilities for retired Air Force couples and widows would never have materialized without the determination and grit of this woman."*[6]

That woman was Helen Maitland LeMay, wife of then Air Force Chief of Staff Curtis E. LeMay. It all began in 1961. After learning of the success of the Army's home for widows and the Navy's proposal for one, General and Mrs. LeMay received many inquiries about creating a similar plan for Air Force widows. Could the Air Force take on such a commitment? Would they? The sheer size of such an undertaking could be overwhelming.

In 1963, Helen LeMay, with the help of the Air Force Officers' Wives' Club of Washington, sent a survey to all OWCs to determine if there was significant interest in such an endeavor. The support of the OWCs would be vital to its success. The response was overwhelmingly in favor of such a project. Helen Maitland LeMay was now ready for the challenge.

Together with Pat Daus, a young Air Force widow, they began the initial stage of an energetic campaign. Pat set up an office in her home in Alexandria and Helen held meetings in her home on Ft. Myer. The AFOWC of Washington continued to support the project and donations proceeded to grow. A

---

6   Metcalf, Jane, *Dowry of Uncommon Women*, p.249.

planning committee was created by General LeMay, and from these humble beginnings the Air Force Village Foundation, a non-profit organization, was formed.

Six years later on May 26, 1969 Mrs. LeMay was present in San Antonio at the Groundbreaking Ceremony for Air Force Village. It must have been a very special day for her to witness the success of such a worthwhile plan. Like all leaders, she didn't do it alone. Air Force officers responded positively to an in-service collection. Ray Ellison Industries generously donated 15 acres for the Village. Industry and government were most cooperative. The officers and the board of Air Force Village worked tirelessly on this project. The efforts of the wives' clubs throughout the world played a major role in its success and their support has continued over the years.

Part of the groundbreaking ceremony included the spreading of soil that had been collected from the bases of 217 OWCs from around the world. The members of these wives' clubs contributed their talents, efforts and time in raising close to a million dollars in just five years. The heart and soul of these women is best described by the words on a plaque given to the Village by the Richards-Gebaur OWC: "Neither distance nor the passage of time shall weaken the eternal bonds of shared experiences and values between Air Force wives."

Air Force Village continues to grow and prosper. Today there is an Air Force Village I and II as well as a resident Alzheimer's Care and Research Center. The mission of the Villages is to provide widows, widowers and retired officers of the Uniformed Services and their spouses with dignified, appropriate and cost effective living options. Financial assistance is provided to needy Air Force widows and widowers who are given priority for residency.

The determination of one person, Helen Maitland LeMay, has contributed to the well being of many people. She had great vision.

Paulette K. Johnson

At the 25th Anniversary Meeting of the Air Force Village Foundation in October 1989, a note was sent to the delegates by the First Lady with the following words.

"...How could anyone not be impressed by the challenge met by the Air Force Officers' Wives' Clubs? The original group of OWC members who saw a need and began work on filling the void exemplifies all that is best in the American spirit. Those visionaries, and all that followed, have created something that does honor to everyone, both in and outside the military family. Both George and I admire and applaud you for your constancy of purpose.

I know you have enjoyed a spectacular week together. George and I send our very best wishes for your continued success in providing dignity and warmth for those who have served us all so well."

Warmly,
Barbara Bush

So Much More About Helen LeMay

"My parents were a good team. Mother had boundless energy and a friendly outgoing personality," says Jane LeMay Lodge, daughter of Curtis and Helen LeMay. For more than four decades, Helen LeMay championed quality of life issues for Air Force families.

In the early days of General LeMay's leadership of the Strategic Air Command (SAC), Helen LeMay was concerned with the inadequate or nonexistent housing for the families in her husband's command. During General LeMay's nearly nine year command, Mrs. LeMay's highest priority was securing modern family housing units for servicemen and their families who were desperate for acceptable places to live. Together they were instrumental in implementing an extensive housing project known throughout the Air Force as Wherry Housing.[7]

Helen LeMay's daughter explains, "She was a doer and was always the one to call on if you wanted something done and done right." Always watchful for ways to improve the Air Force way of life, General and Mrs. LeMay were responsible for the creation of the Family Services Program, a relocation assistance program, now a part of the Family Support Center. And together

---

7   Senator Wherry of Nebraska, the state in which the Strategic Air Command was headquartered, sponsored the Wherry Housing Project. It was the first housing project of its kind for the relatively new Air Force.

they fostered the creation of the Children Have A Potential (CHAP) program for parents of children with special problems.

With the boundless energy her daughter describes, Helen LeMay started the first teenage club at Offutt Air Force Base, decorating it and painting murals on the wall. Being an accomplished artist was only one of her many talents. Another such talent was in the area of entertaining. She is noted for organizing large social functions at a moment's notice. Hollywood celebrities like Arthur Godfrey, Tony Curtis and Janet Leigh came to call on them at the Air House.[8] "It was nothing to have 60 people for a sit down dinner," Jane remembers.

In the 1960s Mrs. LeMay led the campaign for an Air Force widows' home in San Antonio, Texas. She personally wrote to 94 officers' wives' clubs asking for their support and, as word spread, soon had contributions of nearly three million dollars. Her concept evolved into what is known today as Air Force Village.

Even after retirement this energetic couple continued their efforts to support Air Force families. They established The General and Mrs. Curtis E. LeMay Foundation in 1987. The foundation assists "those widows of all Air Force retirees who spent their lives, for the most part, coping with the difficulties of military life without complaint and staying the course."

Perhaps the best way to remember Helen LeMay is through the words of her daughter Jane. "She was an extraordinary woman and indeed the best asset the Air Force ever had." Any mother would be proud to receive such a resounding tribute from her daughter.

---

8   Air House is the official residence of the chief of staff of the Air Force. It is located on Ft. Myer in Arlington, VA.

Few people understand the unbelievable inner strength of Helen Maitland LeMay. But those who do, know full well she is the perfect match for the strong-willed mind-set of Curtis Emerson LeMay.

The preliminaries to the wedding service in the Episcopal church were batted about by the prospective bridegroom and the nervous bride-to-be.

First off, the bridegroom wanted no singing, no rehearsal and certainly he would entertain no thought of kneeling during the wedding vows!

When he told his bride, in no uncertain terms, that he would not participate in a rehearsal, she simply pretended not to hear and had her mother practice the walk down the aisle.

Came the day of the wedding.

The sanctuary of the church was ablaze with the glorious colors of the flowers. The scent of their perfume wafted through the lofty nave.

The church was packed and still there were guests trying to get inside, no matter that there were no empty seats. Six of Curt's brother officers were resplendent in their dress uniforms. The six bridesmaids were visions of angels in their flowing gowns of the palest pink.

The bridegroom, who fully expected his wishes to be observed as law, preceded the best man to the altar only to note the two pink kneeling cushions lying in wait on the step to the chancel. The famous scowl stretched to his jowls. "A high Episcopal mass!" he growled nearly aloud.

Right on the heels of the growl came the tumultuous chords of the organ and in an instant a soprano voice soared out in the dulcet notes of "O Promise Me!" By this time, the bride had arrived and was standing by his side. Instead of the look of love the congregation was expecting to relish, he glared at her with fury darkening his face.

The bride smiled at him demurely.

The service proceeded and the moment came for the happy couple to kneel. The priest spoke softly, "Please kneel."

The bridegroom stood his ground, priest or no.

Again, the priest asked, "Please kneel."

Now Helen knew she must take action. Without lifting the hem of her wedding gown, she quietly kicked this man she was marrying with the pointed toe of her shoe.

He knelt. Relieved, she, too, knelt.

Jane Metcalf, *Dowry of Uncommon Women*

Paulette K. Johnson
Correspondence with Jane LeMay Lodge

Nancy Harkness Love

In the mid-1930s a young woman from a prominent Philadelphia family found a job in Boston selling airplanes on commission. Her long list of customers included Joseph Kennedy, Sr., who, according to one account, was more concerned in finding a wife for a future president, his son, than in buying a plane. The young saleswoman, Nancy Harkness, apparently wasn't interested. She had her own marriage in mind, one that would in its own way gain her local celebrity. In 1936, she married an Air Corps Reserves officer called Robert Love. The union was splashed all over the Boston papers—"BEAUTIFUL AVIATRIX WEDS DASHING AIR CORPS OFFICER" read one headline; "THE ROMANCE OF THE GLAMOROUS YOUNG SOCIETY COUPLE MEETS THE ROMANCE OF THE SKY" announced another. The marriage did more than give Nancy public attention. It placed the already extremely capable pilot in an excellent position to lobby for a women's flying squadron during the war.

Love was the daughter of a wealthy physician; she had been flying since she was a teenager. Though she went to all the right schools, including Milton Academy in Massachusetts and Vassar in New York, she was restless and adventurous. In college she earned extra money taking students for rides in a plane she rented from a nearby airport. Once she flew so low over campus, almost brushing the treetops, that someone was able to read the plane's tail number. University officials were not amused. She was suspended from school for two weeks and forbidden to fly for the rest of the semester.

After their marriage, the Loves built a successful Boston-based aviation company for which Nancy was a pilot. She also flew for the Bureau of Air Commerce: In one project she tested three-wheeled landing gear, which subsequently became standard on most planes. In another, she helped mark water towers with town names as a navigational aid for pilots.

Love was not a headline-grabbing pilot like the famous aviator Jackie Cochran, but her qualifications as a pilot meant that her first proposal for a women's flying squadron, though rejected, was taken seriously. In May 1940, just months after the Second World War broke out in Europe, Love wrote to Lieutenant Colonel Robert Olds who was setting up a Ferrying Command within the Army Air Forces. She said she had found 49 excellent women pilots who could help transport planes from factories to bases. "I really think this list is up to handling pretty complicated stuff," she argued. "Most of them have in the neighborhood of a thousand hours or more—mostly more, and have flown a great many types of ship." Olds was intrigued. He took the suggestions to General Hap Arnold, who turned it down, though not permanently.

According to one account, a chance comment her husband made proved a decisive factor in resurrecting Nancy's proposal. In the spring of 1942, Robert was called for military duty in Washington as a deputy chief of staff of the American Ferry Command. Nancy got an administrative job in Baltimore, to which she commuted by plane. One day Robert happened to mention his wife's daily flight to work to Colonel William Tunner, who was heading up the domestic wing of the ferrying division. Tunner, who at that very moment was scouring the country for skilled pilots, was amazed. He wanted to know if there were many other women who could fly. Within days, he met with Nancy and asked her to write a proposal for a women's ferrying division. Within months, the 28-year-old

Love had become the director of the Women's Auxiliary Ferry Squadron, or WAFS, with 25 experienced female pilots under her command.

From the very beginning, Love and the WAFS had problems getting the media to take them seriously. One of the first newsreel stories showed Love welcoming some of her new recruits. The announcer summed up the story saying: "What will they think of next." *Life* magazine proclaimed that Love was one of the six American women in the public eye who had beautiful legs. The War Department tried to tone down the publicity, urging the press to treat the women pilots with "diplomacy and delicacy." And Love tried to ensure that her pilots did nothing to attract unwarranted attention. She knew that one misstep could turn the tide of public opinion against her whole team. "If the WAFS are to succeed, our personal conduct must be above reproach," she told her recruits. "There cannot be the faintest breath of scandal. Among other things, this means you may not accept rides with male pilots." She went on to explain why. "If a male pilot and a WAF were seen leaving a plane together there would be suspicions that they were playing house in government property."

The following summer, Love was asked to fly an important mission which, if it had proceeded as planned, would have greatly expanded the scope of her operation. The British had asked for the delivery of 100 B-17s in order to fly deep into Europe. Colonel Tunner suggested to Love that she become the first woman pilot to fly a military plane on an intercontinental flight. The day Love and her co-pilot were to set off, General Hap Arnold got word of the mission. Fearing a tremendous backlash if a woman pilot was shot down by enemy fire, he moved immediately to ground the women. As Love started the engine on the B-17 and was about to taxi down the runway, an officer came screeching down the runway in a jeep with an urgent telegram in hand. The message was from Arnold. It read: "CEASE AND DESIST, NO WAFS WILL FLY OUTSIDE THE CONTIGUOUS U.S." Love and her co-pilot shut down their engines. The photographer who was on hand to record the takeoff, took a still of the two women anyway. The picture captures the disappointment of two frustrated aviators trying desperately to smile.

In the summer of 1943 Love's squadron merged with a women's pilot training program that had been set up under Cochran's leadership the previous fall. Cochran was named director of the combined units, which was known as the Women's Airforce Service Pilots, or WASP. Love was put in charge of all WASP ferrying operations. Under her command, female pilots flew almost every military aircraft then in the air. In some instances, they were even asked to demonstrate to the men that a particular plane was safe. According to Colonel Tunner, the women were instrumental in rescuing the tarnished reputation of the high-speed P-39 pursuit plane, which the men had named the "flying coffin." The men, Tunner claimed, were having so many accidents in the ship because they weren't flying it "according to specifications." He ordered a group of female pilots to begin deliveries of the P-39. "They had no trouble, none at all," Tunner noted years later. "And I had no more complaints from the men."

After the war, Love received an Air Medal for her service to the country. She then retreated from public life and raised three daughters. The family moved to Martha's Vineyard, where they frequently hosted WASPs who had been under Love's command. Love died of cancer at the age of 62 in 1976, so she didn't live to see the WASPs being accorded military recognition three years later. But right up to her death, the women she had commanded remained some of the most important people in her life. Among the things she left behind was a box she had kept for more than 30 years. Inside was a handwritten list she had compiled in 1940 of women pilots. It also contained clippings and photographs of each of the women who had died under her command.

Blue Ribbon Panel

In 1987 the Blue Ribbon Panel was created in response to a furor over wives of base-level leaders coming forward with complaints that they and /or their husbands had been told that they were not to work while their husbands occupied base-level leadership roles. This was widely reported in the *Air Force Times* and prompted a firestorm of letters alleging similar experiences.

Secretary of the Air Force Edward C. Aldrich and Chief of Staff of the Air Force General Larry D. Welch issued a statement to clarify this issue. This attempt only stirred the pot. Letters to the editor flew. To investigate and attempt to resolve the controversy, the Blue Ribbon Panel was formed. Its mission was to learn the realities and scope of the situation and to present recommendations.

Under the leadership of Major General Anthony Burshnick, a panel of seven members, a group of consultants, and an administrative and professional support team met at the Pentagon to formulate a plan of action. The result was an itinerary for several fact-finding trips. The panel visited a cross-section of bases, in the US and overseas, to interview Air Force members and spouses. These interviews, approximately 1,100, were conducted over a period of three months.

Every effort was made to balance the interviews so that a valid picture of the issue by rank, command or geography could emerge. As the travel progressed, committees were formed within the group: a committee to draft a recommended policy, a committee to write a report of the entire project, and a committee to draft implementing recommendations. There was a tremendous amount of work involved in this project.

The culminating event of the BRP was a presentation of findings and recommendations to the Air Force chief of staff and the secretary of the Air Force. By this time, Secretary of Defense Weinberger became aware of the scope of the problem through an editorial in the *Washington Post*. As his wife was working, he failed to see the point of those leaders who felt spousal employment was incompatible with a commander's position. He ordered this practice to cease, not only in the Air Force, but also throughout the services.

These findings prompted the adoption of Air Force Regulation 30-51. It states that the choice a spouse makes concerning her private life is indeed that—a private matter, and that decision will not affect the evaluation and assignment of the military member. No longer could the spouse be included in the military member's fitness report. In this day and age it is hard to believe it once was. The panel was also a catalyst in emphasizing the necessity and importance of the Family Support Centers.

It seems unbelievably archaic now that this issue ever existed but it did. The "two for one" concept had been effectively challenged. Perhaps these changes would have evolved naturally because of the realities of increasing numbers of working women. A change in attitude was the only sure way to ensure success. Fortunately, society in general dictated the change.

Source: Pat Thomas, BRP Consultant
Blue Ribbon Panel Reports

Military spouses have a proud heritage of volunteer assistance to their military and civilian communities. Their contributions in clubs, emergency aid agencies, and other family support activities enhance the quality of life in their communities immeasurably. We welcome and encourage their service.

At the same time, increasing numbers of military spouses are seeking full or part-time employment. They contribute to the financial well-being of their families, often gain a sense of accomplishment, and forge links at their workplaces, whether they work in the government or the private sector. As such, they contribute directly to the morale and health of our military members.

It is the policy of the Department of Defense that decisions to seek employment, to be homemakers, and to volunteer, belong to spouses. I am grateful for their energy, their talents, and their membership in the Defense family.

Secretary of Defense Caspar Weinberger
October 22, 1987

Love and Devotion

When I interviewed Mrs. Helen Eubank her husband, Major General Gene Eubank, who was one hundred years old, was present. I was privileged to be in a room with this general and his ninety-three-year-old wife. They had been married for sixty-eight years!

The interview took place in a health care center room at Air Force Village where Mrs. Eubank was recovering from surgery. Imagine that, surgery at her age. She was looking forward to going back to her apartment soon. The two admit they keep each other going and enjoy every minute of it. Mrs. Eubank says, "We do have fun together."

The Eubanks are a legend at Air Force Village. Most of the attention usually goes to Maj. General Eubank who personally knew Orville Wright and was an aide to General Billy Mitchell. The stories he tells are right out of the pages of a history book, and he loves to tell them. But this time it was Mrs. Eubank's turn to tell how she helped young Air Force wives adapt to the demanding Air Force way of life, and how she helped them form wives' clubs everywhere they were stationed.

Helen Kelly was born an Army "brat" on August 28, 1900, at West Point, New York. Her father, Captain William Kelly, was stationed there as a Spanish Instructor. One of her father's assignments took the family to Honolulu, Hawaii. The Kellys were welcomed to their new post at a dinner party held in their honor. The escort chosen for Helen was a young, dashing pilot named Gene Eubank.

Her fate was handed to her because the two fell in love and married. "It wasn't love at first sight; it took some time," says Mrs. Eubank. It was two and a half years before they married in 1925.

Their military life as a couple began at McCook Field in Ohio, a choice assignment for a young flier. Gene was a test pilot. Helen remembers, "That was an interesting place because we were thrown in with all the men who were at the beginning of things in the Air Service…trying out new planes; trying out new ideas." She continues, "General Billy Mitchell was just coming into prominence, stating his views, and causing a lot of controversy."

Mrs. Eubank reminisces about being around such greats as Charles Lindbergh and Orville Wright. She tells a story about Mr. Lindbergh. "It was put in the papers that Lindbergh was going to land. He was always one to downplay publicity, so nothing was said about him. One woman got the news and she arrived out there to see him depart." The woman carried a large bunch of roses and had her little daughter by the hand for this historic occasion. "Lindbergh came walking out to the plane unaware of anything that was happening and she thrust these roses at him. He looked a little alarmed, grabbed the roses and looked around. Standing right close to him was a lieutenant's wife. He pointed at her, gave her the roses and turned around and flew off. Here was this poor woman with her expensive roses and some other woman had them."

As we continue our conversation Mrs. Eubank nonchalantly adds, "From there it was very easy, {and} smooth sailing—except for a couple of wars. We had good stations and good friends and I enjoyed every minute of it."

The most important role Mrs. Eubank played, according to her, was as a senior wife. "I enjoyed the association with the young women I was responsible for." She fell into this role easily because she came from a military family and was familiar with the customs and courtesies. "You feel a great responsibility for them," she explains, "but you don't want to hover over them or try to force your ideas on them. You want to make things as easy for them as you can. It was a great deal easier then, than it is now. The young women were all there, you knew them, you knew their husbands, you knew what they could do, what they would like to do, what they would work at and what they wouldn't. It was very easy. They were anxious to do and to learn and be part of the service." She feels it's different now and admits, "It's much more complicated for the wives. It's just a whole different set-up and I think in many ways we had the easier part."

During World War II, most of the wives worked for the Red Cross. Helen Eubank put in two thousand hours as a nurse's aide. "The Red Cross aide did all the non-professional work of the professional nurse. We made the beds, gave the baths, and oh did we carry bed pans!" The Red Cross program was important since most of the civilian-trained nurses had gone into the service. "It wasn't glamorous," she recalls, "but it was a good program that allowed professional women to do their professional work without having to waste time making beds."

At the end of our interview, I ask how she would like to be remembered. General Eubank answers for her. "By the other women who knew her, she will be remembered as a wife who was always available to help them." Mrs. Eubank replies, "I think that expresses it exactly. Gene has the same devotion among his young officers. They had an affection for him. I think they had a deep respect for his ability and a genuine affection. That's what means so much."

How wonderful it was to witness this loving couple who deeply respect each other and shower compliments on each other before giving credit to themselves. The Air Force is lucky to have such a couple among its ranks.

Sandra Troeber

Helen Kelly Eubank died on January 5, 1998. She was 97 years old. Major General Gene Eubank died on April 9, 1997. He was 104 years old.

A Farewell to the "SAC" Wife

This article first appeared in the Randolph Officers' Wives' Club magazine, the Windicator, *in October 1992. The Air Force at that time was facing reorganization. The Cold War was over and the threat of nuclear war had diminished. The Strategic Air Command (SAC) was dissolved and their planes and personnel reassigned to newly formed commands. "Alert" tours, where crews lived together one week at a time in preparation of an enemy attack, were canceled.*

There are many of us out there. We spent years of our lives as an "alert widow." Every time we heard the klaxon, we wondered, could this be the real thing? We prayed no. The men who left families behind to go to the missile silos left them hoping the button would not have to be pushed. There were the Tanker Task Force TDYs to Alaska, Europe, and the Pacific.

Over the years, we have lost friends and neighbors through Vietnam and airplane accidents. The hours went by like years waiting and wondering who. But we remained strong for the family. When a SAC plane went down, we felt as if we had lost a family member. Another SAC wife was grieving and we felt her pain.

Then there was the alert tour. We were a family whose husbands lived together one week out of every three. We were there with the kids visiting dad. We got to know these families. Our children learned what the Northern tier states were. They saw more snow than most kids see in a lifetime. We made friends with people in places we never heard of, much less thought we might live. No doubt, those people are still are friends.

There was Bomb Comp. For the guys it was a BIG deal. Being number one was what it was all about. There were ORIs and on some bases there was the legendary cookie bus—FREE food, supplied by the wives, for anyone on the flight line working after hours. Anything to keep those airplanes ready and able to fly—safely. Our new language consisted of words like MITO, cell, generation, rendezvous, diverted, EWO, Nav leg, shack, show-time, bus time, crew dog, and rent-a-crowd, just to name a few.

When our husbands left for places unknown, we knew they would be involved, not in an exercise, but in a real mission to protect our country and our world from the grasp of power-hungry countries. We had to be strong, independent, and flexible.

Now we are a part of history—the end of an Air Force era. SAC has been disbanded and has gone the directions of the four winds. But the SAC wives of the years gone by are a unique group of women. Like the official SAC patch, we are out of print, but the legacy remains. I am very proud to have been a SAC wife, part of history.

Gerry Franklin
The Randolph OWC Windicator
October 1992

Traditionally Speaking

*"As wives if we do not know one another,
how will we be able to support one another,
and stand together in times of need?"*

Alma Powell

A Trunkload of Memories

"The modern military wife derives her heritage from the past. She carries with her a trunkload of memories—a legacy. Each generation has experienced the trials and joys of military life and added to the contents of the trunk."

Ann Crossley and Carol A. Keller
The Air Force Wife Handbook: A Complete Social Guide

My experiences as a military spouse have been forged and shaped by those who went before me, countless, sometimes faceless and often nameless women of amazing strength, courage and vision.

Like many of you, my mother is among the military wives who have "gone before," leaving behind a rich and loving legacy. My father was a career NCO in the United States Air Force. He first joined the Army Air Corp at age eighteen and was part of the famous Red Ball Express. When the Air Corp became a separate and integrated service, he was on the very cusp of this exciting transition. Wherever his assignments took him—to coin a phrase—there we were.

However, as a result of my mothers' loving influence, each duty assignment was more than just another assignment, it was home—a place filled with warm memories of friendship, assignments and places we had traveled. As each picture was carefully hung and items of furniture placed just so, our new quarters quickly became home. Each ding in the furniture or missing piece carrying a story of adventure and travel.

Before long, my brother and I would find our way outside to make friends. Among us was always one who either had been to or recently arrived from a place that another was going. Our common experience as "military brats" was the tie that bound us as we became reacquainted or forged new friendships.

My fondest memory however, is of the fragrant aroma of my mother's home-cooked meals, which greeted my brother and me as we came in from play. Sometimes she and the international friends she made abroad would exchange recipes or could be found in the kitchen experimenting. In this manner, I developed an appreciation for other cultures. And to this day some of those recipes remain family favorites. Whether my father's duty orders took us stateside or abroad, we always found friends, some old and some new, at our destination. They were always there with hands extended in friendship and arms opened wide with a welcoming hug as they assisted us in making the transition.

At Ramstein Air Force Base, there were the kaffee klatches and stairwell parties. There were also great base-wide picnics with gallons of barbecue sauce and children playing everywhere amidst the smoke and smells of a home-style "family picnic." It did not matter that we were many miles from "homes of record" or "biological families." What mattered most was that we were together, making memories and forming friendships that would last a lifetime.

The experiences behind each of these memories helped mold me into the person that I am today. I certainly did not hesitate to share my life with a man "on orders." This is the only life I have ever known and without exception, it has been good.

That is not to say that it has been without challenges. I sometimes quip that I am "Air Force bred and wed"; however, that statement is only a partial reflection of my 40+ years of military experience, beginning with my father's enlistment. For more than twenty years, our family traveled the world. When my husband and I met, he was a ROTC cadet. We married in 1978 and in 1979, graduated from Tuskegee University, both wearing brand new 2nd Lieutenant bars. In 1986, following a serious auto accident, I was retired from active duty status. Because of my service and other qualifications, the Air Force paid for me to fulfill a life-long ambition—attending law school. I received a juris doctorate in 1989, clerked for a state supreme court justice and served as deputy district attorney before the "inevitable" orders arrived in 1991.

My husband was selected to attend Air Command and Staff College in residence. I was excited for the opportunity provided him; however, I worried that my career would suffer. For the last eight years I have been a stay at home mom and author. I recently sat for and passed the Texas bar examination, but before I could be sworn into the state bar, the "inevitable" orders arrived. Disappointed? You bet. However, I firmly believe that God has a purpose and a plan for each of our lives. I count it a privilege to have been a full-time mother and wife when my family most needed me. I also believe that God does not close a door without opening a window.

During the time J.R. was assigned to Air Command and Staff College in Montgomery, Alabama, I began writing a historic cookbook entitled, *The African American-Heritage Cookbook*. The cookbook contains the history, recipes, and vintage photographs of Tuskegee Institute (now University), a historic black college founded in Tuskegee, Alabama by former slave, Booker T. Washington. When J.R. was assigned to the joint staff at the Pentagon, I researched the history and photographs, which make this book so unique, at the Library of Congress. By the time he was reassigned to Montgomery to attend Air War College, the book had been published and distributed to bookstores nationwide. Consequently, I was able to promote it throughout the South, but most especially at my alma mater, *the* Tuskegee University. Despite three assignments in five years, all things came together for good. I pursued an interest I might not have otherwise found time to pursue. I am currently studying for the California Bar. Yes, the "inevitable" orders have arrived.

So you see, like the Apostle Paul, I can identify with you on any number of issues. I have been a dependent child of an active duty, professional noncommissioned officer. I have been a professional married to a professional officer; and I am currently a stay at home mom.

This is all part of my heritage, which I derive from my past. I carry a trunkload of memories from those who, in the words of Carol A. Keller, author of *The Air Force Wife* "…have gone, along the wagon trails of the American West and across the jet contrails of the contemporary world. …each generation experience{ing} the trials and joys of service life and add{ing} to the contents of the trunk."

Inspired by the ceremony for fallen soldiers, often performed at formal dinners, I designed a table setting to honor the contributions of spouses. The hand-woven basket, represents the sometimes sparse simplicity of service life and the strength and useful beauty created when our patriotic pride, sacrifice and commitment, is interwoven with that of our spouse, family, and other military families. It represents a pattern of service that has been our tradition for more than two hundred years.

The American wildflowers contained in the basket represent the military spouse, strong and resilient. Found in the most unlikely of places such as high craggy mountainous areas with barely enough soil to sustain them, or dry, sandy barren areas, where nothing else worthwhile seems to grow, the military wife, like an American wildflower, takes root, flourishes and brings beauty to her surroundings.

The coffee pot represents our heritage of hospitality, begun when early wives, who were far from home, in desolate places came together to share a cup of coffee, a favorite recipe, and the burdens of their commitment to service life. The tradition, dating back to those turn-of-the-century army posts, where a shared cup of coffee brought welcome respite, continues to this day. It is our way of saying, "Welcome, you are one of us now, we stand by you—through good times and bad." It is also a way of bidding a fond farewell to old friends, but always, at the center is a circle of friendship and sense of community. The cup is the common cup of shared experience, what one drinks, we all, in a sense, share. It contains a slice of lemon, representing the bitterness of the sacrifice we sometimes are called upon to make. Finally, the sterling teaspoon, containing sugar represents the purity of our love for God, family and country, and the sweetness of love and friendships that helps remove the bitterness from our shared cup.

Carolyn Denise Quick Tillery

It Pays to be Thrifty

The Thrift Shop is a unique volunteer experience as well as a business. The success of that business is tied to the size and commitment of its volunteer force. The "face" of that force has changed in the past decade as more and more Air Force spouses choose to work outside the home.

However, there still exists a strong sense of the value of such an organization to the wives' clubs[9] as well as to the immediate base community. Anyone who has spent more than a day at a thrift shop has seen examples of this.

I have watched young couples faces light up at the sight of a desperately needed crib or chest of drawers…a little worn perhaps, but suited to their budget. I have watched mothers doing back-to-school wardrobe shopping for their children, everything from shoes to back packs. I have helped more than one reservist as he searches the jewelry counter diligently for a special something to take home to his wife or daughter.

People purchase crutches, walkers, portable potties and sometimes an antique. We have opened up after hours for families who have lost everything in a fire and provided quick, inexpensive relief for their immediate needs, not the least of which might be replacement toys for their traumatized children. We have boxed up donated items to send to storm victims here

---

9   The Thrift Shop on most Air Force bases is operated solely by the Officers' Wives' Club (OWC). However, on some AF bases it is a joint operation with the Enlisted Wives' Club (EWC). *Ed.*

and in far away lands and for Kosovo refugees who landed on our very own doorstep.

Volunteering at the Thrift Shop is an absolutely wonderful way to get to know people from around the base and in the retired community. "New blood" from the active duty community is a fact of life, especially after the summer PCSs devastate the volunteer force each year. The volunteers who are retired are an important source of continuity and, in my experience, have been the most incredible ladies.

At Travis AFB there was a woman named Rita Klemas. She was a widow and the Thrift Shop was her life. For close to 15 years, she came in every day the shop was open and stayed from the first hour to the last, and then some. Sorting donations was her favorite job and she created a section we named "Rita's Bargain Basement." Some customers came specifically to shop there.

When her health was failing and she was on the list for a heart transplant, we had to forbid her from coming to work. That had a devastating impact on her emotionally, and we finally relented when a letter from her doctor indicated that her volunteer hours would do more good then harm. I am sure that every Thrift Shop has at least one "Rita."

At McGuire AFB her name is Juanita Russell. She has volunteered for twenty years and is incredibly hard working. Like Rita, she takes particular pride in sorting donations. In the process, she collects items (such as socks and pajamas) which our policy prohibits us from selling, and takes them to a local nursing home where she also volunteers.

Bertha Becker works as the Donation Chairman at the Tinker AFB Thrift Shop. She and Elizabeth Sharpe have worked there for over nineteen years. However, Mary Kruljac still has seniority there with close to twenty-eight years of Thrift Shop volunteer experience.

The "Suits for Success" program at the Tinker Thrift Shop has yielded great results thanks to Bertha's help. The Thrift Shop donates two "interview outfits" to participants in a local job retraining program. When they find employment they come back to the Thrift Shop for two additional work outfits.

The reasons for spending volunteer time at the Thrift Shop are as simple as working to earn money for the OWC/EWC Welfare Fund for scholarships and charities, and as complicated as a lonely newcomer trying to find friends and a sense of community in yet another new home.

Most volunteers, like myself, have more subjective reasons for showing up each week. In a lifestyle that often defines us by our husbands rank or position, the Thrift Shop is a great equalizer. There is work to be done and we roll up our sleeves and do it. Rank has no privileges at the Thrift Shop and often not even something we necessarily know about each other. But we do know about each other's children, joys and sorrows.

We live a nomadic life and the Thrift Shop offers a place to bond with each other and to contribute to a worthy cause. It is an outstanding example of a tradition in the military that we are family not by blood, but by choice.

Karen Spiker

A Class Ring Reunion

While sorting, pricing and tagging donations at the McGuire OWC Thrift Shop one of the volunteers found a high school senior class ring. It had been tucked in a purse along with an earring, key and other miscellaneous items. On it were the initials T.A.M. and the year, 1982.

Another volunteer looked at the ring and noticed it was from a "rival" high school near her alma mater. Knowing that the ring might be of sentimental value to someone, she phoned Cardinal Dougherty High School to see what could be done to reunite the ring and its owner. The school's alumni association thought it was important enough to put a note about it in their newsletter. Eventually T.A.M.'s brother read it and asked his sister if it might be hers. Indeed it was. She had taken the ring to her 15th class reunion and had kept it in her purse. That was in 1997. In 1999 she dropped off some donated items, including the purse with the ring inside, at the Thrift Shop. Until her brother mentioned it she hadn't realized it was missing and probably would not have missed it until her next class reunion.

Thanks to the extra effort and caring of several individuals, T.A.M. will have a wonderful story to tell at her 25th high school class reunion.

Paulette K. Johnson

Remember When

I was unpacking some book boxes in our attic today and it unexpectedly turned into a trip down memory lane. I spotted the familiar red, white and blue cover of a book that was my Air Force Bible. Once again, memories of a different era rushed over me. (I guess it could have been a hot flash, but I think it was a memory.)

The book is entitled *Mrs. Lieutenant.* It was written in 1968, by Edna Frews, and is brimming with military etiquette. I received my copy that same year from my husband's section commander's wife, at our first assignment in Laredo, Texas. She gave a copy to each wife, knowing if we had a dollar we still couldn't buy a clue regarding how to behave as military wives. We were all fresh out of college, partying was our long suit, courtesy and formality was a short club.

Suddenly we had been dropped into a well-established world of ceremony, custom and tradition. A world of right and wrong with very little gray area.

This book served me well for many years and I was thankful for it. But times change! Some of these customs rightfully died a graceful death, and for those I am thankful. However, you might be interested in reading some of the guidance given to new officers and their wives a lifetime ago.

Social   *"You may not decline the New Year's Day Reception unless you are out of town or sick in bed, and then your husband should go without you."*

"You should not place your gloves and bag on the table or tilt your chair to reserve a seat at the Woman's Club luncheon."

Dress   On Hats: *"most women look forward to the opportunity of wearing a sassy creation to lunch. With today's hair fashions, you will not be incorrect if you are bareheaded. In like manner, you will never be incorrect if you wear one. If you are undecided, carry your hat in your hand."*

On Making an Official Call on the Commanding Officer: *"wear a simple dress or suit, with gloves and bag. A hat is optional."*

It used to be a custom that you and your husband called on his commanding officer and his wife within just a few days of arriving at your new base. Calling cards were a must. One with the wife's name was left in the tray and two with the military member's name. Why did the wife leave one and the husband leave two you ask? The wife left hers for the commanding officer's wife only. However, the husband left one for every adult in the household.

This custom gave way to the New Year's Day Reception. It sufficed for the yearly call. It was eventually discontinued because of the expense.

Slacks and *"These are fine on the tennis court or about the house*
Shorts   *on a cute slim figure but are out of place and forbidden at the commissary and BX, theatre and public places. Since today's fashions stress women in pants, try to be discreet as to where and when you wear them."*

Miscellaneous Advice

"Avoid cliques, and gossip."

"Don't be the life of the party."

"Two car lengths should be left vacant at the entrance where a party is being held. One for the senior officer and one for the arrival and departure of other guests."

"Never ask an officer to push a baby carriage or hang out laundry." (I swear that is word for word from the book.)

"Restrict your telephone calls to five minutes....Having long conversations on the telephone is a bad, hard to break habit, but your accomplishments will be greater if you overcome it." (I swear.)

The closing paragraph in the book offers this advice. "Sometimes it is better to do the wrong thing graciously than the proper thing rudely."

Betty Karle

Once Upon A Time

In 1956 Nancy Shea revised the 1951 edition of *The Air Force Wife*. It was dedicated to Air Force brides and was written as a common sense book about Air Force life. Remembering that the Air Force was less than 10 years old, it also served as a guideline to the traditions of this young service.

The advice "Be active socially, and proficient in at least two things, such as bridge and golf, tennis and dancing," is of another era. But her advice that "You owe it to yourself and your family to circulate enough to broaden your horizons. At any rate, set your sights higher than the level of the kitchen sink," is perhaps Nancy Shea's inspiration for things to come.

Paulette K. Johnson

Airman's Attic

The Airman's Attic gives young airmen a start in their new home by providing them with needed household items free of charge. All this is done with donations and the dedication of volunteers. On most bases it is a part of Family Services and the Family Support Center. In some cases the First Sergeants' Association supports it.

This story is written by a spouse who breathed new life into an otherwise static "attic."

I've never known anything but the military. I was born into the military and swore that I would never have anything to do with it. Then I met a handsome cadet at the Air Force Academy. We have just celebrated our twenty-fourth anniversary, and I love being a military spouse.

I feel very fortunate to have had the opportunity to live in many different parts of the country from Selma, Alabama to Grand Forks, North Dakota. Now, we are on our way to Guam. Even though packing up a house every two years is getting a little old, I wouldn't trade the friendships we've made for anything. That's one of the things I would have missed if I weren't a military spouse. I have walked away from every assignment with a sense of pride knowing that, even as one spouse, I made a difference. I have seen what military spouses can do. Airman's Attic at Whiteman AFB has been my biggest contribution and my way of "making a difference."

When we arrived at Whiteman I thought I would like to try and expand my volunteering experience. The Airman's Attic needed an advisor, so I jumped in with both feet. That was before I knew what I was getting into!

The Attic, located in the back of the Family Support Center building, had concrete floors, cinder block walls, racks and racks of children's clothes from the 1970s and 1980s, a couch with one leg missing, a rocking chair with no arms, metal shelves piled with "stuff," mismatched everything, dead bugs and dust, dust, dust!

Cleaning was the first step. Thank God for friends. Armed with buckets, gloves and rags we washed down everything in sight and threw out broken and old items. Civil Engineering helped build shelves, lay carpet and replaced the metal front door with a recycled glass door. What a big difference a little light makes. After several weeks we were ready for business.

Next step was recruiting volunteers. My efforts focused on the young wives who were our customers. "Tell your friends about the Attic," I said, "and help me recruit volunteers. If we could get this Attic off the ground," I explained, "it would help all the young airmen." They knew first-hand how rough it was to make ends meet. Childcare for volunteers was provided and all workers would have first choice of donated articles. All items were free of charge. What incentive!

The third step was getting donations. A furniture store in Sedalia donated recliners, couches, and love seats. A thrift store in Warrensburg donated children's clothing. One class at Airmen Leadership School had a drive for the Attic to increase our inventory.

Soon people realized our needs. Only household items, furniture, children's clothing, uniforms and maternity clothing were accepted. The base paper ran an article, and once the airmen saw that we had things they really could use, the word spread fast.

A customers' wish list was created to identify items that the Attic didn't have. A few people have taken items and returned them when they didn't need them any more. One airman brought back a couch after he was able to purchase a new one.

The Attic is open several days a week and averages twelve customers per day. It is run almost entirely by airmen's spouses. We are proud of our newly renovated Airman's Attic that is now fully operational and running like clockwork. It took a lot of blood, sweat and tears, but as I look back it has all been worth it. I tell others, "Don't be afraid to jump in and get involved. I highly recommend it!"

Jerri Schoeck

You've Got Mail

Destination White House. Before the alarm rings I am out of bed and downing a cup of coffee. Today is the day I join the Air Force spouses who volunteer weekly in the mail room at the White House. I am "pumped."

Every Friday a group of spouses from the DC area travel to the nation's capital to participate in the White House Volunteer Program. This Friday I am joining them and I feel like a teenager heading to a rock concert.

Most of us meet at the Anacostia Metro Center to journey downtown together. Once there, we descend on a local coffee shop for breakfast "to go" and walk the rest of the way to the Old Executive Office Building, known as the OEOB, to begin the day. All the volunteers have a "V" badge, which allow them access to the building. I am issued a temporary pass. The necessary paperwork and security check had been done earlier.

Walking into the OEOB is like walking into a new school—the corridors are large and impressive—the atmosphere almost reverent. The OEOB is a gorgeous building right next door to the White House, and it is steeped in history. It once housed the Department of State and War Department.

Not far from the security check is the mailroom where we gather around a large table piled with stacks of letters and all the supplies we would need. Jim Reagan, who has worked with this group for years, is waiting for us. Time to begin the day and sort (not read!) the president's mail. On this Friday we have quite a bit of mail and we jump right in. I am overwhelmed by the fact that I am sorting mail addressed to the president of the United States—something to tell my grandchildren.

Mail is arranged by type. There are letters, requests, literature, pictures, donations and some are written in foreign languages. Envelopes with only "The White House" for an address have had no problem reaching their destination. Jim is quick to help if there are questions. Mail addressed to the First Lady and those written by children are sent to designated offices. In rooms scattered throughout the OEOB, volunteers are busy gathering requests and answering mail. This job could not be done without their help. Volunteers must complete an application, sit for an interview and pass a security check. A commitment of sixteen hours a month is requested.

It has been almost ten years since Air Force spouses started volunteering in the mailroom of the White House. The group changes in size and membership but their enthusiasm never wavers.

Today it has taken almost five hours to sort the mail. We leave knowing we contributed in some small way to the smooth functioning of the executive branch of our government. We bid farewell to Jim, walk through the security checkpoint and are off to a late lunch. Tonight I will write in my journal about my wonderful experience.

It was all I knew it would be.

Paulette K. Johnson

Mother of the Groom

"Wear beige and keep your mouth closed." That bit of wisdom was given to me whenever I asked other mothers of the groom for advice. It was usually the only piece of advice given to me.

Planning a long-distance wedding is not uncommon anymore. For military families it probably is more the norm. It can be even more complicated if the prospective bride and groom each live in different cities. Often miles separate other siblings and immediate family members too.

Dealing with geographical separations is nothing out of the ordinary for military spouses. We've been doing that long-distance communication thing for a long time. If we could give birth alone, travel across country with the children and the family pets, and buy and sell homes while our spouses are deployed, this couldn't be hard. Little did I know that keeping my mouth closed would be harder than all the above.

Phone companies, computers and the Internet have made it easier to become involved. For "wedding-challenged" families that's good news AND bad news. The good news is I can make long-distance calls for five cents a minute. No more "wait until after five" calls for me! Cell phones add a new dimension. And e-mail is free! The bad news is, not only do I have to practice keeping my mouth shut, I must also learn to resist the urge to use my keyboard.

Nevertheless, technology has become a valuable tool for planning a wedding. I can look up web sites for hosting a rehearsal dinner, use my fax machine to receive contracts, listen to demo tapes of musicians and bands, buy invitations, and order monogrammed napkins and flowers over the Internet. All take a wide range of credit cards that make it easier to spend money than you ever thought possible. You can even arrange for you and your wedding guests to order photographs of all the festivities on-line!

When my son became engaged, I immediately searched the inventories of on-line booksellers for books written for the mother of the groom. Although there were hundreds of wedding books listed, I could locate only one specifically written for the mother of the groom. And it was out of print. Was there a message there?

The second piece of advice given to me came from a photographer who was enlarging some of my son's baby pictures. My son's fiancee requested these for their engagement party. I asked for 5 x 7s because I thought the black and white photos wouldn't look good enlarged to 8 x 10. Ever so cautiously he asked me what the bride-to-be requested. Hesitantly I said, "an 8 x 10." Gently he said, "Take my advice and do what your son's fiancee asks. It will be well worth it." I followed his advice, wondering what I was thinking in the first place. The point is—I wasn't thinking. Being sensitive to her wishes was something I needed to work on. This whole event was becoming an exercise in self-improvement!

The third pearl of wisdom came from a very experienced source—my 80-year-old mother. She said, "Try not to give any advice. They usually figure it all out without your help anyway. It just might take a little while." It was my mother's tactful way of saying, "keep your mouth shut." However, now I noted I must add patience to my growing list of needed virtues. There must be a twelve-step program for mothers of the groom!

"Letting go" would be the key to survival. It wouldn't be just "letting go" and letting these two wonderful and very capable adults make their own decisions, it would include "letting go" of my son too. That would be the really hard part. For some reason we all recognize this time for the mother of the bride but seldom address it for the mother of the groom. Mothers and sons have special bonds too.

Of course throughout this "letting go" period, and up until the wedding week, the wonderful spouse I married will probably be deployed, TDY, or involved with some very special time-sensitive project. Often wedding plans are compounded by a change of duty station, military crises, and maybe even a retirement. I knew a military couple who were married by proxy when the bride and groom were separated by unexpected orders. I guess I should consider myself lucky.

At times it will be difficult, but throughout this process I'll try to remember some other advice I read a long time ago: "There are two special things you can give your children— roots and wings." The roots are the fun part. The wings— wings of their own—are the hard part.

Paulette K. Johnson

Bee Arnold, wife of General Hap Arnold, tells this about being the mother of the bride at the marriage of their daughter Lois to Ernie Snowden. "Whether we liked it or not, they were going to be married on the 20th of December, but we did put on a wedding with six bridesmaids and a maid of honor. It was a very funny thing, we drove to the little chapel, and they left me in the car to go down the aisle just before the wedding, and then forgot all about me. The wedding march was sounding and, 'where's mother?' So I hustled in there, and they held back the wedding march until they got me in place.

Colonel Murray Green, USAF Ret
Interview with Mrs. Bee Arnold
August 22, 1970

What is a Commander's Spouse?

- Commander's spouses may come in any shape or size. They may be short, tall, or thin; she may be blonde, brunette, redheaded, or bleached, while he may be graying or bald. However, they must always be "well-rounded!"

- They may be people watchers, aerobic dancers, librarians, soccer or softball coaches, bluebirds, scuba divers, or above-average golfers.

- They most assuredly are peacemakers, diplomats, social secretaries, bookkeepers, committee persons, hostesses/hosts, counselors, or sports fans...and possess a ton of energy.

- They are ambidextrous and have the ability to look blank, interested, intelligent, and aghast...sometimes all at the same time.

- They are multi-lingual and have the ability to decipher the quiet mutterings or verbose ravings of a stressed-out spouse after a particularly trying day.

- They can be deceptive too, for they can look back upon these rantings without batting an eye when someone states what a placid, calm, and disciplined spouse they have.

- They are efficiency experts, for although their spouse must spend countless hours with other people; they have to see to it that "commanders" have time for a few quiet hours with their own family.

- They are tutors, correctors, critics, ambassadors, dictators, helpmates, stalemates, consumers, and collectors.

- They are people to whom many have turned, and have never failed to be there when needed.

- They have seen places most of us will never see and have viewed these through the eyes of tolerance and understanding.

- They have walked with people who are making history and yet have shown concern for every man and woman they have met.

- Their careers have been the Air Force and they have continually demonstrated their love of country and pride of the military.

- The USAF is a better organization because of their efforts, and their support has strengthened our organization. Their positive attitude is a vital part of the USAF.

- Commanders' spouses are paradoxes: they are active individuals and solitary ones. They have attended countless civic affairs, speeches, innumerable military functions, club meetings, changes of command, and dinners…yet many nights are spent just worrying or waiting because something or someone has priority on their spouses' time.

Author Unknown

Awards and Decorations

"To love what you do and feel that it matters—how could anything be more fun?"

Katherine Graham

Wings of Our Own

"Off We Go into the Wild Blue Yonder..."

Most people recognize the title of this article as the first line of "The Air Force Song." However, most do not recognize the name of Mildred Yount, the Air Force spouse who played a role in selecting this song for the Air Corps.

Below are portions of an article written by Colonel Murray Green, USAF-Ret., entitled "Off We Go Into the Wild Blue Yonder..." that appeared in The Retired Officers' Magazine *in July 1987.*

In 1937, war clouds gathered over Europe, as Tin Pan Alley might phrase it. Brigadier General H.H. "Hap" Arnold, U.S. Army Air Corps, persuaded his boss, Major General Oscar Westover, chief of Air Corps, that airmen needed a musical expression of their separate identity. How about a song competition with a prize for the winner? A good idea, but the Air Corps then lacked any control of its own budget strings. Bernarr MacFadden, magazine publisher for the masses, came to the rescue. *Liberty* Magazine would offer a $1,000 prize to the winning composer. Not a lot of money, even for those depression days.

Arnold's modest concept included a volunteer music committee chaired by Mildred Yount, wife of Brigadier General Barton K. Yount, Air Corps training commander. Other members included Hans Kindler, National Symphony Orchestra conductor; Rudolph Gans and Walter Nash, all distinguished musicians in their own right.

The song-writing contest attracted no less than 650 entries, including one offered by young Meredith Wilson, whose mature compositions were still some time in the future. With appropriate lyrics, his "76 Trombones" might have made a run on the winner's circle.

The judges were given two years, until July 1939, to select four or five finalists from which a winner might be chosen. As the weeks and months passed, the word got around Washington that none of the entries to date had set the committee on its collective musical ear.

As the July 1939 deadline approached, the music committee's deliberations had produced no clear winner. Then, literally out of the "blue yonder," Robert Crawford—"The Flying Baritone," his friends called him—buttonholed Mildred Yount, urgently seeking an interview. The date was July 13. Crawford offered to sing for her a song he had composed, but just carried around in his head. Mrs. Yount was reluctant. The competition rules called for a manuscript to be submitted with each entry. But, as Crawford was enthusiastic and persuasive, she listened and was electrified by what she heard.

Mildred Yount sat Crawford down and made him record the words and music on a blank score sheet. To be fair to the other contestants, she slipped Crawford's rough manuscript, "The Army Air Corps Song," into the middle of the pile the committee would review two days later at their final meeting.

His entry was an instant and unanimous selection, a verdict good enough for Arnold, who set in motion plans to give the song exposure and invited Crawford to perform at the Cleveland Air Races during the coming Labor Day weekend. Crawford kicked off each day's activities with a rendition on the public address system. He also performed on a national radio hookup.

At the final inaugural ball on Saturday night, September 7, Crawford received his $1,000 check from MacFadden, and brought 700 diners to their feet, cheering, when he concluded his rendition with a fortissimo flourish, "...and nothing can stop the Army Air Corps!"

Evidently, there was not enough money to underwrite copywriting and publishing, so Crawford arranged with Carl Fischer Inc., a New York music publisher, to handle the song, with a performance release in perpetuity executed in favor of the U.S. government. Thus, the Air Force today, unlike the Army, Navy, and Marine Corps, does not own its "official " service song.

Post-World War II, as the service gained legislative co-equality with the Army and Navy, Crawford modified the lyric: "...and nothing can stop the U.S. Air Force."

Colonel Murray Green, USAF, Ret.

SKYLARKS (skȳ'larks) noun.   *1. larks noted for their song while in flight. 2. group of Officers' Wives' Club members on Air Force bases who enjoy singing together and performing for various organizations. Their history is almost as long as the clubs they represent. One of their special performances is recounted below.*

"The United Services Organization was holding a celebration for Bob Hope to thank him for his USO shows overseas, and they were looking for a women's choral group," explains Betty Ramsey. "A friend of Bill's (her husband) suggested the Skylarks. I guess everyone thought it was a good idea because it wasn't too long before we were all climbing aboard Air Force buses and traveling down to the USO building in Los Angeles. There, we met our musicians, the Marine band from 29 Palms. We practiced together briefly at the USO, and then it was back on the buses again."

"The celebration was held at Bob Hope's house at Taluca Lake," Betty continued. "It was a two-story brick home and just off the family room downstairs was a courtyard, which was where we performed. For our opening song, we sang 'Thanks for the Memories.' Both Bob Hope and his wife, Dolores, sang it with us. It was quite moving."

Veronica Nelson
LaPetite Roche, Little Rock AFB, OWC
May 1987

The General & Mrs. Jerome F. O'Malley Award

The Air Force T-39 Saberliner overshot the runway during landing and plunged down an embankment. On board were the Commander of Tactical Air Command, General Jerome F. O'Malley and his wife Diane. It was only four days after their thirtieth wedding anniversary. Friends and family were waiting at the Wilkes-Barre Airport. General O'Malley had a speaking engagement that night in his home state of Pennsylvania. The date was 20 April 1985. All five aboard perished in the impact.[10] The Air Force and several Air Force families suffered a shocking loss.

After their parents' death, the O'Malley children, James, John, Margaret and Sharon, established an award in memory of their parents. It recognizes the wing commander and spouse whose contributions to the nation, the Air Force, and the local community best exemplify the highest ideals and positive leadership of a military couple in a key Air Force position.

Chief of Staff General Ron Fogelman said on the tenth anniversary of the award, that it honors a couple "who display similar commitment [as the O'Malleys] to Air Force values and quality of life."

---

10 The three others killed in the crash were Capt. Harry L. Haugh, pilot: Lt.Col. Lester F. Newton, co-pilot; and TSgt. Robert A. Eberflus, the aircraft's crew chief.

As a tribute to General and Diane O'Malley, and to those who have won the award, a plaque with the names of the recipients is hanging in the Pentagon.

At the tenth annual award ceremony at the Smithsonian Air and Space Museum, the O'Malley children presented a painting to the Air Force. It was the first time all four O'Malley siblings could attend the ceremony together and their gift was a stunning portrait of General and Mrs. O'Malley. The artist has captured their spirit on canvas. General O'Malley has his arm around his wife. The painting's vibrant colors intensify the subjects' dazzling smiles. If you hadn't known them, you wished you had.

The painting is displayed in the Pentagon at awards presentations. Also in the Pentagon, encased in glass and displayed on a wooden base, is the O'Malley trophy—an elegant crystal Falcon with outstretched wings poised in flight. The plaque and trophy are all located in the Air Force chief of staff's corridor amidst other prestigious Air Force awards.

Once a year the office of the Air Force chief of staff honors a wing commander and his or her spouse for their exemplary service. Many deserving couples are nominated. All are exceptional leaders and spokespersons for the Air Force. Listed on the following page are those who have been so honored.

Paulette K. Johnson

The General and Mrs. Jerome F. O'Malley Award

1986	Col. & Mrs. Peter D. Robinson
1987	Col. & Mrs. Ronald W. Iverson
1988	Col. & Mrs. Ben Nelson, Jr.
1989	Col. & Mrs. Ronald G. Shamblin
1990	Col. & Mrs. Joseph F. Mudd
1991	Col. & Mrs. John M. McBroom
1992	Brig. Gen. & Mrs. Fredrick D. Walker
1993	Col. & Mrs. Roger R. Radcliff
1994	Brig. Gen. & Mrs. Bobby O. Floyd
1995	Col. & Mrs. John H. Campbell
1996	Maj. Gen. (Sel) & Mrs. John R. Dallager
1997	Brig. Gen. & Mrs. Robert C. Hinson
1998	Brig. Gen. & Mrs. John R. Baker
1999	Brig. Gen. & Mrs. Steven A. Roser
2000	Brig. Gen. & Mrs. Robert D. Bishop, Jr.
2001	Brig. Gen & Mrs. Gregory H. Power
2002	Brig. Gen (Sel) & Mrs. Douglas L. Raaberg
2003	Brig. Gen (Sel) & Mrs. William A. Chambers
2004	Brig. Gen & Mrs. Dana T. Atkins

At the Turn of the Century

Did you know that in 1999…

- Approximately 352,536 individuals were on active duty in the Air Force.

- 63 percent of Air Force members were married….
  — 74 percent of the officers and
  — 61 percent of enlisted personnel

- Active duty Air Force members supported 523,155 dependents.

Joan Orr
Spouse of the Year Award

"They Also Serve..."

"*Total commitment to the Air Force way of life. Ora Spencer is the hard working, behind-the-scene spouse we all know. If you need something done, she's there. If you need a volunteer, she's there...A role model to military and civilians alike...A champion for our youth...She neither seeks nor wants personal recognition—exactly why she so richly deserves this award.*" Those are but a few of the words used to nominate Ora Spencer for the Joan Orr Spouse of the Year Award in 1998.

Once a year the Air Force Association honors the recipient at their national convention in Washington D.C. This award is a tribute to the late Mrs. Joan Orr, the wife of former Secretary of the Air Force, Verne Orr. Since 1987 the award has recognized spouses for their significant contributions to the Air Force. A plaque in the Air Force chief of staff's corridor in the Pentagon lists the names of all those who have been honored. Three words, "They Also Serve...." are proudly etched on the plaque.

To be eligible for the award the nominee's husband or wife must be serving in the Air Force (active duty, guard, or reserve). Military members are not eligible. Nominations describing the spouse's contributions to the Air Force are submitted to the Air Force chief of staff's office.

The AFA spouse of the year in 1999, Norma Holland, was a key organizer of the "Holiday Share/Angel Tree" program at Randolph AFB, a family advocacy counselor and a member of the base chapel choir.

In 1996 Melissa Hagan was recognized for her support and volunteer hours primarily aimed at helping children and young adults. She spent close to 50 hours a week working with troubled teens and with charitable organizations. Melissa was also named Mrs. Alaska in 1995.

Thousands of spouses qualify for this award. Thousands deserve it. Ultimately only one is selected. The honoree is truly representative of all those who volunteer to make the Air Force a better way of life for all. Most, like Ora Spencer, do not want the accolades. Most do what they do out of a personal commitment to helping others. All make a difference.

One special night and one special plaque in the Pentagon gives only one special spouse modest recognition. But by bestowing this honor on one, it increases the awareness of the collective "gift" of all spouses to the Air Force family.

In 1997 Rachel Stahl was recognized for her contribution to the RAF Lakenheath, England, community, including her involvement in the Reading is Fundamental program and serving as president of the Enlisted Spouses' Club.

A spouse from Scott Air Force Base, Patricia Peek, was 1995's recipient. The line-up of Patricia's accomplishments is very impressive. The Airman's Attic, PTA and base programs for parents and children are some areas in which she made a significant contribution.

Following is a list of those who have been honored to receive the Joan Orr Award. One small plaque. One very large collective contribution.

Joan Orr Spouse of the Year Award Winners

1987	Mrs. Ann E. Triplett
1988	Mrs. Linda S. Allen
1989	Mrs. Rita C. Szpila
1990	Mrs. Brenda J. Kramarczyk
1991	Mrs. Leigh P. Culver
1992	Mrs. Kim J. Kozlowski
1993	Mrs. Loretta J. Lindsey
1994	Mrs. Margaret A. Hebert
1995	Mrs. Patricia G. Peek
1996	Mrs. Melissa R. Hagan
1997	Mrs. Rachel E. Stahl
1998	Mrs. Ora M. Spencer
1999	Mrs. Norma H. Holland
2000	Mrs. Maureen M. Arceneaux
2001	Mrs. Lorisa S. Pinder
2002	Mrs. Charlotte D. Engeman
2003	Mrs. Tammie Lynn Bocook
2004	Mrs. Sandra L. Rodriguez

Spouse Day

Since 1984 the military services designates a day to recognize the many contributions of military spouses. Secretary of Defense William Cohen designated May 14 as Military Spouse Day in 1999. He said, "These women and men face many challenges as they manage the unique demands military life places on them and their families. Dealing with deployments, family separations and frequent moves requires special skills and commitment. Throughout the history of this country, military spouses have proven they are up to these challenges."

Paulette K. Johnson

Touched by an Angel

Angels come in all shapes and forms. Heroes, neighbors, parents, friends, and even strangers. They are selfless, courageous, humble, dedicated and much more. How do you show these "angels" that you appreciate them? How do you thank them?

Eunice Welch, wife of then Chief of Staff of the Air Force, General Larry Welch, found a way. Mrs. Welch recognized that the quality of life in the Air Force was enhanced by the volunteerism of its members. Many of the support services would be crippled without the help of those volunteers. Neighboring communities also benefited from base related participation.

Her inspiration came in the form of a small gold angel pin perched on the shoulder of another Air Force spouse. With determination and a gentle spirit, Eunice Welch began an Angel Award program to recognize volunteers. Commanders' spouses were asked to encourage participation in this effort. And so in 1987 the Angel Award program began to spread its wings and fly.

Recognition, not regulation, was the theme. Each base was given the flexibility to adjust their program to fit their needs. Some chose for bravery, others for dedication. Some chose one recipient for the year, others chose several. Some awards were given only to retirees and dependents; others included active duty members and civilian personnel. Some even chose groups of individuals.

All were presented an angel. Initially these beautiful gold cherubs were purchased from a jeweler in Thailand. Sponsorship of the program was generally the Officers' Wives' Club or

Enlisted Wives' Club. Participation was widespread. In later years the wing or base commander adopted the program. On some bases the Family Support Center presents the award during National Volunteer Week, which is traditionally the third week in April.

In 1993, Connie Yates, wife of General Ronald Yates, then commander of Air Force Materiel Command, boosted participation in the program and encouraged establishment of guidelines and procedures on Air Force Materiel Command (AFMC) bases. The Family Support Centers in AFMC serve as the community focal point for the program. The pin design was changed to a pair of wings with a halo on them.

Eunice Welch is very much an angel herself. Today she is still helping those in need and volunteering her time to local and Air Force communities. The Welches' home is adorned with angels, most given as gifts. Each has a story behind it. One room has dozens of angels gracing the walls. When you enter it you can't help but smile.

Volunteers have touched our lives in many ways. Eunice Welch helped us to recognize some of them. Look around you. Are you standing next to an angel?

Paulette K. Johnson

The Gift that Keeps on Giving

Spring 1992...Castle Air Force Base, Atwater, California has just been notified it will be closing within the next three years. "Downsizing," the current buzz word of the 90s college textbooks, and BRAC (Base Realignment and Closure) has just hit home. It is more than the usual military transfer....it is the closing of an institution, a way of life, a historic landmark. Castle Air Force Base stands proudly as a hallmark to the men and women responsible for the B-52 and KC-135 "school-house."[11] It is the end of an era.

Within the scope of the base organizations was the Castle Officers' Wives' Club. Founded in the 1940s, it evolved into a dynamic, philanthropic organization that contributed to the well being of the base and its surrounding community. With the imminent closure of the base, the OWC refused to expire silently. They would make sure Castle's memory lived on.

Closing an OWC was a relatively new experience for most of its members. Where do you start? How do you preserve history and create a legacy? With dedication and determination, the Castle OWC set out to do it right. Advice was sought after from bases that had already gone through the process and from the base Staff Judge Advocate (JAG).

In disposing of assets, the OWC wanted to maintain their spirit of community support, while preserving the name of Castle Air Force Base. Creating an educational endowment

---

11 B-52 and KC-135 flight training squadrons were located at Castle Air Force Base in California.

fund fulfilled these criteria, and nearby Merced College became the chosen recipient.

The purpose of the endowment, under the management of the Merced College Foundation, would provide scholarships to deserving students. Recipients would be military members, veterans, retired military members, or their immediate family members. The student must be involved in student activities and/or community service.

The OWC far surpassed the minimum requirement of $5,000 to initiate the endowment. By June 1994, over $16,000 was presented to the college's president. Since the creation of the fund, the endowment principal has grown significantly and thousands of dollars have been awarded to many students. This perpetual fund assures that deserving students will continue to benefit from the club's generosity and foresight.

Closure is never easy. The death of an organization carries its own unique personal meanings and yes, a very real sadness. But the OWC of Castle Air Force Base refused to disband with just hugs and a ceremony. The endowment that they provided

Spouse Scholarships

The Aerospace Education Foundation began its Air Force Spouse Scholarship Program in 1995. Approximately thirty, $1,000 scholarships are given yearly to Air Force spouses seeking a graduate or undergraduate degree.

In 1997, the AEF established the $500 Janice R. Whittle Memorial Scholarship. Whittle, an Air Force spouse, requested that part of her estate be donated to fund a scholarship for spouses of Air Force personnel holding the rank of E-4 or below.

It is another gift that keeps on giving, and an example of one AF spouse helping another.

Paulette K. Johnson

is testament to the proud history of those who had served at Castle since the 1940s.

Air Force spouses ensured that the name of Castle Air Force Base would not be forgotten. They include Melinda Schuck, Jane Pierre, Jacquelyn Thompson, Debbie Bishop and Tracy Neal. But the money for the scholarship fund would not have been raised without the volunteer work and fund-raising efforts of its members throughout its 40+ years in existence. Because of their efforts, the name of Castle AFB will be remembered long after the sound of airplanes has disappeared.

Carolyn Stegman
Paulette K. Johnson

Lights...Camera...Action

"My first experience with role-playing was as a refugee begging for food and water. The scenario took a couple of hours to complete. It was a great deal of fun and I was hooked!" That is how Jane Walsh describes her part in a training exercise in a Phoenix Readiness class.

It all started when her husband Terry asked if she was interested in volunteering at the 421st Air Mobility Squadron at the Air Mobility Warfare Center. He mentioned he could use some help during some of their field training exercises.

During this class, Terry, who was usually an instructor, would actually work with the "Opposing Force" team in scenarios specifically designed for the course. "Volunteering," Jane pointed out, "meant I would actually get to role-play alongside my husband." Since the instructors often worked long hours during these training classes, she looked at it as a chance to spend some quality time with him. "How could I not say yes?" she asked. "The opportunity to see first hand what went into training was too good to pass up."

Before she knew it she was wearing an enemy uniform, carrying and firing M-16s and AK-47s, riding in humvees and role-playing numerous characters. She's played a drunk, a refugee, a host-nation journalist, an international reporter and an accident victim with an amputated arm.

Eventually Jane's volunteer work extended to Phoenix Raven, a training course specifically created for security policemen. During these exercises, she played the part of a terrorist, a utility flag person, an angry mob member and a pilot. Most recently she paired up with the one and only female student for one-on-one physical ground fighting.

Ms. Walsh confides that, "The opportunity to participate in military exercises as a volunteer is not only a privilege, but very rewarding too." She admits that playing various roles has not only been a great deal of fun for her, but has allowed her to meet many fascinating people from across the country and overseas. She adds, "Anytime I can help I don't hesitate to join in."

"Most importantly," Jane says, "I have a greater appreciation for my husband and what it is he does when he heads to work each day."

On January 13, 2000, the spotlight focused on Jane Walsh as she received the Civilian Volunteer of the Quarter award at the McGuire AFB Quarterly Awards Recognition Ceremony. She was honored for providing key training for Phoenix Readiness team members by helping them learn to survive and protect DoD resources in hostile areas around the globe.

In February 2000, the Air Mobility Warfare Center selected Jane as their Civilian Volunteer of the Year.

Paulette K. Johnson

Creating Our Own Path

"The future belongs to those who believe
in the beauty of their dreams."

Eleanor Roosevelt

Wings of Our Own

Isn't It Romantic

Merline Lovelace didn't realize she was conducting research during her exciting, adventure-filled career, but when she hung up her uniform in 1991, she decided to combine a love of romance with a flare for story-telling, basing many of her tales on her experiences in the service. As a career Air Force officer, Merline spent twenty-three years in uniform. During her years in the military, she met and married her own handsome Air Force hero and stored up enough adventures to keep her fingers flying over the keyboard for years to come.

Much like her characters' stories, fate played a part in her entering the Air Force. She hadn't planned on entering the service and had even sent her trunks off to grad school, which was to start the following week. She says, "But after a chance encounter with a recruiter at a lunch counter, I decided to try the military first, and THEN go back to school. I told him I'd either head off to Lackland that week or it was no deal. He made it happen."

She goes on, "Similarly, while in the military I never turned down assignments or special tasks. Each new experience/assignment was a chance to learn. I find the same holds true in writing—each book is an adventure, a chance to explore another setting or culture or profession. I do lots of research and try to take the reader into the adventure with me."

Since retiring, her keyboard's been clattering as she produces one action-packed sizzler after another. She now has thirty published novels, many of which have made the *USA Today* and Waldenbooks bestseller lists. Over four million copies of her works are in print in more than two dozen countries.

When asked to comment on her accomplishments she says, "I follow a very simple formula for success—JUST DO IT. If I'd stopped to think about whether I could command a wing or write a book, I probably wouldn't have had the nerve to try either. But I didn't worry about whether I could, just gave it my best shot."

In addition to her string of highly successful romances, she also authors mainstream thrillers. These action-adventure novels, all with military settings, blend fact and fiction, intrigue and romance in a highly combustible combination.

Merline has won numerous honors and awards, and five of her books have been nominated for the Romance Writers of America's prestigious RITA award. She's particularly proud of the fact that the University of Oklahoma named her the 1998 Oklahoma Writer of the Year, adding her name to a roster of literary luminaries that includes Louis L'Amour and Tony Hillerman.

Contrary to the misconception that there is a "formula" for writing fiction, Merline's found that each book is individual and distinct. In fact, she's discovered that the profession of writing is much like her Air Force career—challenging, incredibly hard work, and great fun.

When asked what her biggest challenge has been, she answers, "Keeping a balance in life. This held true during my Air Force days as well as in my writing career. I tend to dive in and give a job or a project everything I have. I have to force myself to come up for air, and remember that there are more important things in life than deadlines—-like husbands and families and walking in the rain." She admits her best strength is her incurable optimism. "I see life as a great, joyous adventure. Throughout my career, I looked forward to every PCS and the opportunity to explore new places and make new friends. Even in the darkest moments—and there were some—I tried to remember that the night always passes and the sun will shine again."

After sharing one war, two exciting careers and three decades of adventure and romance with her husband, Al, she unabashedly admits he's the love of her life and the role model for the hero in every one of her books.

Paulette K. Johnson
Source: Interview with Merline Lovelace

Cyberspouses.com

Only a few years ago, whenever my husband received orders, one of us would immediately head to Family Services to check out a packet with information about our new base. This was my only introduction to our new home, unless I was lucky to know someone there, or was given an enthusiastic sponsor.

Have times changed! In seconds, from the comfort of my home, I can tap into the Internet and get all kinds of information from official and unofficial web sites. Air Force Crossroads at www.afcrossroads.com covers a wide range of helpful topics. Family Support Centers allow you to view the web site version of their SITES (Standard Installation Topic Exchange Service) booklet at www.dmdc.osd.mil/sites. It lists information on housing, childcare and base facilities and services. A new web site, Military Acclimate at www.militaryacclimate.com helps you project moving expenses and forecasts the cost of living at your new location. And MAPS, the Military Assistance Program at www.dod.mil/mapsite, will help you with your job search and provides links to other valuable sites.

Moving isn't the only reason to access the net. If I care to share information or ideas with someone from another base I can post a message or join a chat room. Several of these sites are operated, owned and/or managed by Air Force spouses. At several sites I can locate the latest military pay chart, gather PCS data and share information. Poems and stories about military living are available at many sites. Several Air Force spouses have established chat rooms. Others have created web sites to keep in touch with friends and family, especially when overseas. Recently several women started publishing *Military Spouse Magazine*, a periodical for military spouses. Their web site is at www.militaryspousemagazine.com.

Many spouses of members of the other uniformed services also offer support. For example, Sgt. Mom's military family support web site, at www.sgtmoms.com is managed by a Navy spouse. Another Navy spouse, Dr. Paula Sind-Prunier, known as the Career Coach, can be found at the Military Spouses Career Network at www.mscn.org . If you are looking for information about the job market, go to www.milspouse.org, the web site jointly sponsored by the Department of Defense and Department of Labor.

Interested in what's happening in Washington, DC? The National Military Family Association (NMFA) representing the seven uniformed services can be reached at www.nmfa.org. Want to find out what the best buys are at the commissary? Just type in www.commissaries.com. If you are seeking information about military spouse scholarships you can find the details at the Aerospace Education Foundation web site at www.aef.org. The age of technology has opened a new world void of bias or prejudice. "It's gender, demographics and background blind," says Elizabeth Fetter, president of NorthPoint Communications. Managing computer sites or web pages can be done at home on a flexible schedule. And it is mobile; your family's address may change, but your web page doesn't have to.

Spouses can look for support and information as well as friendship on the Internet. Try several search engines. Google's site is easy to follow. Just type in "military spouses" and get ready for a tidal wave of data. "Bookmark" your favorite sites for easy access. There are links and web rings that will take you around the world or spin you in circles. Some offer assistance in creating your very own web page.

Years ago I was able to read everything available about our new duty station in less than an hour. In this age of information I can surf for hours at a time.

Paulette K. Johnson

(Note: At the time of publication the web sites listed above were easily accessible. However, in the fast paced world of technology, some sites may have moved locations and changed their addresses without notice.)

Teaching—A Noble Profession

Margaret Weinzettel has had an adventurous life. She has devoted a career to education, spent some time in the Navy, and is an Air Force spouse.

After graduating from high school in 1925, Margaret went to a teacher's college for four years and started working in the mountains of Virginia, then later moved to the Richmond area. She preferred to go about teaching in rather interesting ways. For example, the seventh grade social studies curriculum required the study of Virginia history, as well as local history. However, her county didn't have any recorded history, despite its being one of the oldest in the state. Accepting that as a challenge, she and her students set out to write it themselves. Margaret explains, "We happened to have a cooperative superintendent who let us have a school bus to ride around in and read tombstones. Each student then found the oldest person in their vicinity to go out and interview and find out the old stories and legends." She admits, "Back in 1932, this was considered very unusual."

Margaret left the teaching profession for a while to pursue other interests but returned when asked to become a supervisor. She jumped at the chance and credits her good fortune to her creativity and unique teaching methods. In-service training was her specialty for the next seven years.

Then, when World War II broke out, she felt an itch to get involved. "Word got around that I was dying to get into the military," she recalls. "The Navy had a place for me because they needed people with an education background to help in production of training films."

Margaret quickly learned about discipline and says the Navy did more for her than she did for it. She continued in the production of training films until the war was over. When she ran into an old friend, Roy Weinzettel, her life changed paths again. Margaret separated from the Navy, and she and Roy eventually married. In 1948, the couple went to the Philippines for their first assignment as husband and wife.

Because Clark Field was so new, there were no schools. Asked to put her exceptional educational background to work, Margaret organized classrooms and curriculums. Her goal was to establish an accredited system; General MacArthur's office set the standards. They built classrooms out of Quonset huts. She recruited some of the talented, qualified wives stationed there and turned them into teachers. They formed classrooms for nursery up through high school and proudly graduated the first high school class of five.

In 1950, Roy was reassigned to Washington, D.C. to work for the CIA. Margaret wanted to continue teaching. A superintendent she had known in Virginia was now in the D.C. area and welcomed her with open arms. They offered her a school principal position in Arlington, Virginia. Again, she jumped at the chance.

After an assignment to Kansas, the Weinzettels were then sent to Wiesbaden, Germany and Margaret immediately got involved with base activities She joined the American Women of Europe where she was in charge of hospitality and protocol, and became chairman of the wives' club. She enjoyed these new learning experiences.

They returned from Europe in 1958 and went back to D.C. and the Pentagon. Margaret returned to the same school in Arlington where she had been principal and joined the supervisory staff. In 1961 both Margaret and Roy retired. After living in Florida and North Carolina for many years they moved to Air Force Village in 1976.

Margaret believes that life is governed by your attitude. "If you have the right attitude toward life than you take your bumps as they come, you rationalize and accept them."

Through teaching Margaret has influenced many young people. One day she received a letter from a friend who had been stationed at Clark Field with them. Their child had attended the high school Margaret started. In the letter the woman said, "I'm sitting at the bedside of Andy right now. He lies in traction. He had polio as a child and they didn't know it until he became an adolescent and one side (of his body) didn't develop like the other. I was just sitting here at two o'clock in the morning remembering what a wonderful influence you had been on him when he was at school in the Philippines. I just wanted to tell you about it."

Once again, she knew she had taken the right path in life by becoming a teacher.

Sandra Troeber

Standing Her Ground

You can say Cindy Shaners is a typical American homemaker. She works during the day and spends time with her family at night. Her free time is spent dedicated to her hobbies-making dolls, painting picture frames and stopping slap shots. For the past two years, this military family member and mother of two has joined the fast growing number of women hockey players.

Cindy Shaners' interest in playing hockey started while stationed at Elmendorf AFB, Alaska. With her husband Tech. Sgt. Dave Shaners, the couple spent many nights watching the Anchorage Aces, a local minor league hockey team.

At each game, Cindy focused on the goalie.

"The goaltender is the least recognized position on the ice," she said. "When a team scores a goal, they congratulate the scorer. They never congratulate the goalie when a shot is blocked."

After months of being a hockey spectator, she decided to make the long transition to a hockey player. Cindy, who had never set foot on an ice rink, traveled to the local sports shop, purchased all the equipment necessary to be a goalie, and joined the local hockey league.

For the three months she was a member of the Puck Junkies hockey team, she avoided concentrating on statistics and standings so she could focus on learning the fundamentals of the sport.

Being the only woman on the team didn't cross her mind either.

"All of the men on the team treated me just fine," she said. "They were all good sports—they treated me like one of the guys."

The only thing holding her back she said is her own "personal demons." Her age, skill level and lack of experience. I wish I found the game earlier in life, she said.

While her new career on the ice was going well, a permanent change of station assignment to McGuire (Air Force Base in New Jersey) nearly ended it all. They unpacked their hockey equipment, eager to begin their lives in the northeast—a region known for its passion for hockey—but they were disappointed McGuire didn't have a team of its own.

The Shaners weren't about to give up their newfound career so they decided to start the McGuire Falcons, a team in the Medford Adult Hockey League. They went around base looking for players, recruiting about 20 people for the team.

Dave credits the development of the team to his wife. "She is the backbone of the team," he said. "Without a goalie, you don't have a team."

On opening night, Cindy will once again be the only woman on the team. Although this is a role she is used to, she hopes one day she can see more women on the ice.

Tom Crosson
McGuire AFB Airtides
March 12,1999

Writing as an Afterlife

Almost from the beginning of my husband's many years in the Air Force, I found a home for my own talents in wives' club publications. Throughout the years, those of us who worked on the magazines bemoaned the fact that books about military wives had little connection with the reality of how we lived. "Someday, someone ought to tell it the way it really is" became a kind of staff mantra.

When one more service-wife-fantasia was published at the time "we" left active duty, I decided what I wanted to do in my "next life" was write. At a workshop for writers, Lee Roddy, creator of TVs Grizzly Adams, advised that I would learn more about free-lancing at a writer's camp. There I decided the route to writing a book was to begin with articles.

My first published pieces were profiles of women whose lives or work I admired. Then, I met author and National Public Radio commentator Tom Bodett of "leaving the light on for you" fame when sitting next to him on an airplane. I wrote, requesting an interview, to which he agreed. After that, there was no turning back.

The six articles I published on Bodett led to others for editors of the newspapers and magazines I worked with in that process. Since my husband and I were also traveling extensively as a result of his business and our far-flung family, he kept urging me to share our experiences in travel pieces. It wasn't until we'd visited Ireland that I was moved to try my hand at it.

After that I wrote of our visit to Berlin the year after the wall had come down. Other pieces have included Maui,

Brussels, Belgium, the Oregon Dunes, our own tiny but historic town of Steilacoom, Washington, the North Cascade Loop and a host of others. I developed a West Coast network of newspapers that publish my work.

When I requested an interview with internationally famous glass artist Dale Chihuly, I was amazed to be asked to pick up this man they call the Tiffany of modern art glass at the airport and drive him back to his studio. Although he wears an eye patch ever since he lost the sight in one eye in a car accident some years ago, he volunteered to drive so that I could record the interview en route. My only fears were of messing up a great opportunity. *US Air Magazine* and *Seattle Magazine* were among the many who bought pieces that sprang from our time in the car and over breakfast that morning.

I choose and research my subjects and travel destinations based upon what I think will interest a particular publication's readers. Whether I am venturing into an area about which I know very little or a great deal, I always precede interviews and articles with research in libraries and on the Internet. I want to be prepared with enough background to ask intelligent questions. Interviews of experts often provide input for articles.

For example, before I did a story on separation and reunion during Desert Storm, I interviewed couples and numerous psychologists involved with military family issues. I want to be sure to get hold of the latest information about whatever subject I'm tackling. If it is a travel piece, I try to ferret out new or unique places to stay, eat or visit wherever we may be. This is especially important because travel book information is often outdated by the time it is published and periodical articles allow travelers to gather more current tips. Even for those who will not travel immediately—or ever—the article should allow the reader to see, taste, smell, hear and feel what the writer experienced. Many times readers will cut out one of these articles and show up a year later in a place I've written about, clipping in hand.

Some of the most difficult pieces I have done were for *Women's World*, because they require they be written on a fourth-grade reading level. Given that, it was also great fun to research a psychologist's view of "The Seven Secrets of Everlasting Love," to share tips on moving that I had garnered over the years and to pass on how even young children can learn to save lives in an emergency.

Many of my articles center on the subject of art or artists. As a result, I have done quite a few pieces for *The Artist's Magazine* and have also been assigned regular Arts and Entertainment pieces for a West Coast newspaper. Many of the artists I write about are the wives of retired military.

With a hundred pieces in print, I find articles have become a kind of addiction. But I'm also back at work on the book that started it all. In many ways it too is a travel story— about the taste of a dust storm in the Texas panhandle, the chant of an auctioneer hawking tobacco down the lane from the converted garage apartment that was "home" for six months in the Carolinas or the rows of shiny, tasseled corn stalks that stand like plumed sentinels in the fields of southern Illinois: all that a military wife sees, hears, tastes or touches on her singular journey through life.

Why I Stay

I was amused recently by an article in *Air Force Times* about the retention problem. One of the reasons men gave for leaving the military was that wives now have their own careers. Once established, wives refuse to move because they don't want to abandon jobs and seniority.

In an effort to offset this powerful influence, the article described the Air Force answer: open houses for wives so they can see how important their husbands' work is. Obviously another male solution dreamed up to solve a woman's predicament.

Why was I amused? Because it is just such tunnel vision that creates some of our problems. Perhaps it is an adequate halfway measure—it is important for a wife to know what her husband is doing in order to appreciate his tensions, to understand his world. It is important in any job, any family.

But I don't suppose it ever occurred to the powers-that-be that retention might be better served if the men themselves and their commanders visited the places where the wives work, so they might see the important things women are doing in their lives and careers.

Despite letters of appreciation and toasts "to the women without whose support," I suffer some resentment when I realize that I am recognized only in my supporting role. I am loved for "keeping the home fires burning" or "supporting our efforts" —or, ironically, for merely surviving my husband's TDY, rather than being credited with growing because of it.

I am certainly not asking for special favors for wives, only that the military have a token awareness of me as a complete and independent individual. It is not the "importance" of my husband's job that makes me adjust to the military life. It is a myriad of intangibles that have much more to do with my independence than with my "dependent" status.

It was that story about open houses, that nudged me to rethink the reasons I am still a military wife. I can answer poetically:

> It is the man, of course,
> But that goes without saying.
> He's the reason I'm, here—
> But not why I'm staying.

Why are we both here after so many years? Certainly if I had hated this life, we wouldn't be here. Why we are here centers very much on me and on our family, because there were other choices: getting out or splitting up.

I ask myself why when friends complain or get out, cutting their ties with no regrets. Many of them will be lost as friends as our lives diverge. "We don't have anything in common anymore" is not just a myth. What is it that they hate and we love? What makes it worthwhile for us and torture for them? Why do their complaints seem like advantages to us?

I asked myself why in a class I recently took called "Death and Dying." Almost all my classmates (all from the civilian community) talked about how they'd never really thought about dying. I realized then that my life is different.

I don't ask myself "If," as they do. I ask "When?" When my husband is later than I expected or the radio reports an "unconfirmed rumor of a missing airplane," I hear my heart beat faster or catch myself sighing unexpectedly. I hear the house so silent with the waiting that it is hard to swallow.

I listen for the Volkswagen van—or for the blue car with "U.S. Air Force" on the side. The "surprise" for me will be the two of us sitting together on a porch some 20 years from now, rocking away to the beat of dancing grandchildren.

I have steeled myself for the day when I must gather my forces within me. I await the expected. It doesn't hang heavy over me, but I am always aware. That alone is reason enough to ask why I am here.

I am here for a hundred intangible reasons, and none of them has to do with the "importance" of my husband's job except, as it is important to him.

I am here for that weekend we had together in Athens. Or in Madrid. Or in Hong Kong. Or in the New Mexican desert. I am here because in the middle of a TDY he will call and say, "I miss you. We have three days off. Jump on an airplane and come."

That same awful TDY strengthens me. "It's a man's work" is an excuse that doesn't work for me anymore, an excuse for not making the effort to learn how for myself. There is a personal thrill of self-reliance resulting from being left behind. Paneling a room or fixing a broken lock or changing a tire or driving to Arizona or even building a cabin are no longer "man's work"—if indeed they ever were.

They are my work—and my satisfaction. I can sell cars and houses, balance checkbooks, and make decisions that can't wait—without crying or calling my mother. I can handle broken legs, strange diseases, stalled cars, broken furnaces, new towns and foreign countries. Certainly these capabilities are not liabilities.

I have taken classes, worked on degrees and traveled everywhere—with and without him.

Am I the only woman who loves the leaving as much as the living? Am I the only one who cleans best when we are going and the house is empty, so the residue of our well-filled lives won't be the gossip of the neighborhood? Surely I am not the only one who never regrets.

Surely I am not the only woman who cherishes being alone, who never feels lonely because it is a shared aloneness. I am not alone in our house and he alone when he is TDY; we are together at each place in shared thoughts, experiencing and enjoying so we can say, like children. "Look what I did while you weren't here."

Beyond that, I cherish my moments alone for other reasons. I experience a special awareness, a special vividness when I am alone. I concentrate on that cathedral or that book in a way that is somehow different when we are together. When we are together, I see it through "our" eyes, responding to what he sees too; when I am alone, I feel that cathedral or book in my personal, unique way.

I have it both ways.

Surely I am not the only one who thrills at leaving a memory-filled and well-loved home with a fireplace in the bedroom and trading it for another house with a bay window overlooking an English pub or a small house with rice paper doors and tatami mat floors. There is such a challenge in getting on an airplane to Nowhere and making Nowhere into Home. There is a special joy in the knowledge that home has been so many places, that our lives have broken into chunks of unique and wonderful experiences.

Our lives do not blend into years of sameness. Each place seems to bring out a different facet of ourselves as we concentrate on something new. In one place, we are athletes, climbing mountains and riding bikes. In another, we are sophisticated city dwellers attending concerts in the park.

In yet another place, we are carpenters and architects, remodeling an old home or building a cabin. In another, we are students finishing up degrees, we are political creatures becoming active in the local scene.

Having lived so many lives, I am like a cat, but I do more than survive my nine lives—I live them.

There are even special joys in working in my unambiguous way. I don't look for career progression as much as career-broadening experience. We will be settled soon enough. Every job lasts but a year or two, and I always leave because "my husband was transferred." What a convenient excuse for changing jobs and finding something new. I never have to say, "I want to quit because I've met the challenge and it is time to move on," even if it is true.

I am a wanderer, a jack-of-all-trades. I am not unlike my husband who, under the umbrella of the Air Force, has been all things: enlisted man and officer, instructor and student, servant and commander, master planner and dreamer.

I don't resent housewives or professional working wives or volunteer wives or "wives club wives" because, depending on the time and the place I have been all of them, and I don't feel the "pressures" of being evaluated as part of my husband's rating because I disregard those pressures as imaginary.

I am here then because, just as we take from each place, we leave pieces of ourselves behind as well. We are remembered in the leaves of a tree we planted, in initials marked in wet cement, in growing heights recorded on garage walls, in our name on a baby's tombstone in another land.

I am here for the friends who drop into New Mexico for a visit on their way from Nevada or Colorado.

I am here, finally and most importantly, because my husband puts us first—not in amount of time, certainly, but in depth and caring. Because we have promised each other Forever and the military only promises Maybe. But it is a good Maybe, a strong Maybe that promises choices and changes.

And so when military leaders wonder why we stay, they should remember the intangibles. Don't insult me with quick-cure answers like open houses and the importance of my husband's job.

Give me credit for being here for reasons all my own. Yes, continue to answer my questions when I ask and be available when I need help.

But don't patronize me. I'm a big girl now.

I know why I'm here.

Ms Beck
Reprinted with permission of Army Times

As for the word "dependent" it's official—it no longer exists in the military! In February 1994 the Department of Defense tossed it from its jargon when referring to a military mate, acknowledging that it was perceived as derogatory by wives who see themselves as anything but.

Lydia Sloan Cline
Today's Military Wife, 3rd Edition

"I'm With Her"

"I was having the time of my life as a volunteer," Patty Wilson recalls about her work in the White House Visitors Office. "Little did I know how much fun I was about to have!"

While volunteering in the East Wing of the White House, Patty was offered a staff position in the visitors' office. As a member of the White House staff she supported and attended many wonderful White House events and functions. On some occasions she was strictly an invited guest. One of those special occasions was a farewell gathering Mrs. Clinton was hosting for a friend. The friend was retiring and had been by the Clintons' side since President Clinton was Governor of Arkansas.

Patty remembers, "I was honored when the First Lady's personal assistant called to invite me to a party in the Clintons' private residence." Besides President and Mrs. Clinton, there were about twenty other people at the party. "I felt a little out of place at this inner circle event," Patty says, "but the woman who was retiring had specifically asked for me to be included."

Another special and very proud moment for Patty was being appointed the point of contact for the historic China State Arrival Ceremony, honoring Jiang Zemin. She worked closely with the White House Social Office, the State Department, military offices, federal agencies and departments (FBI, CIA, Justice, Transportation) and the Secret Service. She points out, "I learned so much!"

One of the rather pleasant twists to working at the White House was the reversal of roles between Patty and her husband, Bill. It was now his turn to be referred to as, "spouse of..."

" Invitations would arrive addressed to Mrs. Patty Wilson and Guest. Patty says Bill enjoyed this role reversal and at social functions took great pride in saying, "I'm with her."

Of course THE event to end all events for the visitors' office is the White House Easter Egg Roll, and Patty was looking forward to working on it. "When I joined the staff I knew I wouldn't be there too long—something about being married to an AF guy gave me a clue," she says. So when Bill's assignment came down a few weeks before Easter, she wasn't surprised. But, as always, Bill was very supportive and offered to take leave to move their household goods and meet her in Georgia after the event. So for her last two weeks at the White House, Patty became the Deputy Events Coordinator for the 1998 White House Easter Egg Roll. It was a perfect ending to a very special time in her life.

Patty has great photos and mementos to remember her days at the White House and admits, "It was a wonderful and unique experience."

Paulette K. Johnson

Have Job Will Travel

"I have yet to hear a man ask for advice on how to combine marriage and a career."

Gloria Steinem

Mobility. Flexible hours. Job satisfaction. Opportunity to pursue other interests. Independence. These are just a few of the reasons many Air Force spouses have chosen interesting and sometimes atypical careers. Military spouses have discovered that moving doesn't always mean they have to give up their job. Although at times it is not an easy journey and certain roadblocks may arise, most take the challenge in stride. Along the way new skills and experiences are added to their résumé.

Most find that being in charge of their career helps them balance their lifestyle, broadens their skills, and, ultimately, makes them more productive. A few spouses who have found their special niche in the workforce are described below.

Rebecca Day: Realtime Captioner

Rebecca is responsible for ensuring that various TV shows have live captions to aid and assist the deaf and hearing-impaired community. It involves writing at speeds in excess of 225 words per minute on a stenotype machine that is hooked up to a computer and then forwarded to TV stations nationwide. This is done for all live broadcasts, such as national and local news, as well as sporting events.

Rebecca says, "It is a very rewarding career knowing that you are helping those who are less fortunate than yourself."

Wende Berryhill: Artist

After various volunteer jobs using her creative and artistic skills, Wende began working as a commercial artist for home-builders. Eventually, because of her connection to the Air Force, she ventured into the area of aviation art. Her first sketches were of the KC-135, the plane her husband flew. Soon her artistry, coupled with her framing business, became so successful she converted their garage to a studio. This home business has also allowed her to enjoy her role as a mother of five.

The Berryhill Collection of art and custom-made artwork focuses on all aspects of the military and family life and adorns the walls of many service families.

Jan Hogle: Motivation Facilitator/Performance Consultant

"I will wait in a long line to see any presentation Jan Hogle gives," one spouse had to say after attending one of Jan's seminars.

An Air Force spouse for thirty-two years, Jan enjoys sharing her time management skills with other spouses in a course entitled "First Things First." In addition to time management courses, she teaches a variety of quality awareness, leadership and management development, and team building courses to both civilian and military organizations.

Rebecca Ryburn: Professional Photographer

For almost twelve years Rebecca has been taking portraits. Before her son Matt was born she was a shutterbug focusing on travel and scenic shots. One Christmas her husband bought her some studio lighting and a photography business was born!

Starting out, she photographed children of friends for cost. She proclaims, "I got practice; they got mostly good pictures of their kids." Rebecca adds, "Even though my business has suffered from our many military moves I've learned a lot about my trade. I've had to look for new avenues to use my photo skills. It has helped me stay fresh." She's photographed Little League teams, children's dance troops, high school yearbooks and a church directory.

Kathy Cosand: Air Force Reserve Officer; TWA Pilot

Wish it, dream it, do it. That's the philosophy behind Kathy's busy lifestyle. Kathy is an Air Force spouse, mother of two, a Lt. Colonel in the Air Force Reserve, a C-141 aircraft commander, and a TWA 767 first officer. All that responsibility requires a lot of commitment and organization. And Kathy is a pro at it.

What enables her to manage such an active schedule? She says, "I prioritize, take one day at a time, and don't overdo." "It also helps," she continues, "to have a mate who understands what you want to do." On many days Kathy changes roles several times. Being organized and staying focused keep her challenged—and she loves it.

Paulette K. Johnson

Triumphs and Challenges

"And life is what we make it,
always has been, always will be."

Grandma Moses

Tragedy in the Heartland

It is amazing how quickly a life can change. When I heard and felt the explosions at the Alfred P. Murrah Federal Office Building fifteen miles away from my Midwest City home, I knew instinctively that something terrible had happened. Since that time, I have felt, as so many have, a wide gamut of emotions associated with this tragic event. When the magnitude of the bombing became clear, many people rushed to help. I too wanted to assist in some way but didn't know how. I am a Registered Radiographer and when the need for Radiographers was announced, I knew what I had to do. I was very apprehensive, and a bit scared, but I made the call. My story covers a two and a half-week period following the bombing when I volunteered at the Office of the State Medical Examiner.

It is very hard to put into words my thoughts and feelings since April 19, 1995. I was on the team who x-rayed the remains of the victims. As the reader can imagine, this was not an easy task, physically or emotionally. The work in the coroner's office was different from the other actions tied to this tragedy. While the rescuers downtown worked feverishly and heroically around the clock with the hope of finding survivors, our team began its initial work with the grim reminder of the finality of a madman's work.

The medical examiner's task was threefold: identify each victim, determine the actual cause of death, and find and preserve any evidence that was present with the victim or related to their injuries. Even in that investigative environment, families of the victims should be comforted to know how well their loved ones were cared for while with us. We all went about our tasks with great concern and respect, always mindful to preserve the dignity of each of the deceased. That care and professionalism was paramount in our work each day.

Amidst this somber work, I felt some powerful positives each day. The people assembled at the medical examiner's office were some of the most dedicated, brilliant and talented people I've ever met. The medical and law enforcement personnel worked hand in hand in support of each other to complete the excruciating daily tasks. All those involved were compassionate to their fellow workers and we watched out for each other's emotional well being in a sincere and caring manner that created a bond between us that I have never felt before. It may be one of life's ironies that I may never see some of them again. Because of our shared work, I'll surely never forget them.

In the face of the stark reality we faced each day, coping was difficult for all of us. It was uplifting to see and read all the cards and letters that lined the wall of the main hall. We also had wonderful people who came to keep our spirits up: many who prepared and served meals to nourish us physically and many who nourished us emotionally by listening and counseling when we needed to talk.

We had a unique approach to keep us focused on our mission. When a victim was identified, their name, age and the date was placed on what we called our "memorial wall." A tree was planted, and we placed a blue ribbon on a branch for every person identified. This small acknowledgment of a life lost helped us remain focused on our work with a firm understanding that our efforts were for the public officials investigating the crime and, perhaps more importantly, to aid the families.

It was a special honor and privilege for me to serve the victims and their families, and to have worked side by side with an extraordinary group of people—you all know who you are. If I am ever faced with like circumstances, I would not hesitate to volunteer again. I, like many others around the country and in this great state of Oklahoma, will never forget. I will carry these days with me as long as I live.

"Never again shall they know hunger or thirst, nor shall the sun or its heat beat down on them, for the Lamb on the throne will shepherd them. He will lead them to springs of life-giving water, and God will wipe every tear from their eyes."
Revelations 7: 16-17

Nancy Smith

Mrs. Mayor

Bobbie Freeman was elected mayor of Choctow, Oklahoma on April 9, 1999. On May 3, 1999, a devastating tornado hit the town, causing 3.2 million dollars in damage. At first she thought, "What have I gotten myself into?" But, always the optimist, Bobbie helped her town face this "act of God" and view it as an opportunity rather than a curse. "No one was hurt," she told them. "This is a chance to rebuild and to grow."

The residents of this small town (population 10,000) outside Oklahoma City, are no strangers to adversity. Once before, in 1945, the town was shattered by a tornado, and the bombing of the Alfred P. Murrah Building in April 1995 is still a painful memory for them.

If anyone can rally a town to accept a challenge it is Bobbie. She is colorful, energetic and full of determination. Ask anyone who knows her. "I am not afraid of dealing with problems. I set goals, put them on paper, and then mark them off as I accomplish them."

Bobbie's journey to the mayor's office began just before Christmas about nine years ago. Noticing that the town plaza had no decorations and no Christmas "spirit," she went to a Chamber of Commerce meeting and told them "There is no sign of Christmas at the plaza." Concerned, she continued, "It's depressing. How can the merchants sell Christmas items if their customers are not in the right frame of mind?" The Chamber was impressed with her remarks and told her if she could raise money, they would match her dollar for dollar to buy holiday decorations.

No problem. Fundraising was something with which Bobbie was familiar. The Officers' Wives' Clubs had provided her with plenty of experience! She got busy, organized a bazaar, and raised over one thousand dollars. The next year Choctaw proudly decorated their town. The Chamber took note of this feisty woman, and after several positive contributions to the community, soon encouraged her to run for a position on the City Council.

Campaigning wasn't new for Bobbie either. On several Air Force bases she had run for and served on several OWC boards. She credits her years as an Air Force spouse with giving her the courage and the ability to jump into the political arena. "Being an Air Force spouse taught me how to be organized," she explains. "I had to be. Butch (her husband) would go off to work, and I had to get the children settled and the house up and running. As a spouse," she continues, "I also wanted to get involved and get to know people. I still do."

After eight years as Councilwoman Freeman, Bobbie won the mayoral race. Her position as business development officer for a local bank, along with her role as mayor, enable her to focus full time on the city's growth and development.

Although Mayor Freeman's term began with a huge responsibility, she welcomes the challenges of her elected position. "It's exciting," she says. "I enjoy doing my job every day. I can see the effect of all my hard work."

There is no doubt Bobbie's leadership is producing results. Along the way, her accomplishments and past experiences have enabled her to grow and develop as a person too.

Paulette K. Johnson

Hope on the Battlefield

"We live in a world full of survivors. It proves this world is sometimes a challenging place to live. The challenge can come as an illness, unreconciled relationship, or inner struggle."
— *Author Unknown*

It is what we do with our challenge and how we channel it that counts. Remember—Hope is present in every challenge.

When we discuss a war so often we forget the victories and defeats that occur which make the war worth remembering. Often when I describe my "war" with cancer, people don't notice the smaller battles, their victories and defeats that define it.

I write about my war with Leukemia so people will understand why I say, "Cancer was the best thing to happen to my family and me." We now appreciate the wonderful life God gave us. We celebrate life to the fullest. Often we tell people, "Life will never be the same for us. Nor do we want it to be." But, I believe for you to understand the victory, you must hear about the battles.

The battleground is set on a twenty-nine year old military wife, mother and workaholic. She had no appreciation of her self, son, husband or family. What seemed important to her was having the perfect house, job, money, clothes, friends and projecting the image of the perfect military couple. Who would have guessed that on this perfectly healthy body the grounds for a most devastating war would occur?

The beginning shots were fired in December of 1997, when the perfect military couple, after many years of underlying stress, decided to have a convention of the minds. The wife felt the husband neglected her and cared more about his military career. He was constantly TDY and did little around the house while she worked two jobs to make ends meet. She was angry at the third uprooting in less than seven years.

Each time they moved it was she who gave up friends, a job, and community connections. He was given everything. The military provided him job security, new friends at the shop, and community acceptance because he served his country. Was it fair that she always pick up the slack?

He argued that with every move she became a little more distant. She seemed to work a little more and have less time for him and their son. So he went TDY when he could. And why not? At least when he left for a while there was no conflict. She seemed happier when they took time and talked on the phone while he was away.

After a return from an extended TDY he decided it would be best for the two parties to split. He asked her for a separation. She was completely caught off guard. She felt defeated and retreated to her home to care for her "brokeness."

But the battles didn't end, they escalated instead—the child, the money, the custody, the house, family problems, etc. Finally, conflicts were never discussed or given time to heal because it turned into an all out war. And pride accompanies war, neither side giving in, both fighting until the bitter end. The breakdown and demise of not only a marriage, but of individual selves was imminent.

Even in desperation there is hope. The atomic bomb, Leukemia, was dropped on us in late February. In a routine exam, preparing me to enter the civilian community, the doctor discovered an abnormal white blood cell count of 60,000.

Believing it was part of the tremendous stress I was under, I wasn't worried when they asked to see me in internal medicine the following day.

I remember asking the doctor, in a joking fashion, what was the worst case scenario. When he stated he thought I could possibly have a form of Leukemia, I thought for sure the lab had made a mistake. I can remember putting my head in my hands and praying, "What more can you take from me now Lord?" With my marriage destroyed, I felt surely that I could lose no more.

I called my husband to ask him to come get our son. I was very upset and when he arrived I told of my being ill with flu-like symptoms. I thought all the fatigue, night sweats, nausea, leg swelling, and blackouts were a possible mental and physical breakdown from the stress. He asked if he could remain at my apartment that evening. We have never been apart from that night forward.

The evening of "the bombing" a "friend" came to my "camp" to listen and share in my fears. My "friend" never left my side and went with me the next day to the doctor. When I arrived at the hospital my white blood count was up to 80,000. They immediately sent me to a civilian hematologist, who discovered that my white blood cell count had gone to 100,000 in less than three hours.

I was hospitalized and a complete bone marrow biopsy confirmed that I had Chronic Mylegeniouse Leukemia. The odd thing about the entire ordeal is remembering how hard my husband took the news. I can vividly remember the two of us huddling together. We were worried more about each other than ourselves. Forced to share this grim reality, our mutual respect and love for one another grew. No war would separate or divide that.

I spent several weeks in the hospital trying to get my white blood cells under control. My parents, brother and sisters, all visited. This long line of military children all rallied to my aid in less than twenty-four hours, travelling from all parts of the world.

Each time a family member would visit they assured me everything would be all right. Regardless of the situation we would handle it as a family. As a result, I can honestly say that I never felt alone in fighting this war. Someone has always been by my side, always giving me hope, never letting me waiver in my belief that I could and would win. I guess you could say that my parents really created an elite group of soldiers. They truly defined loyalty.

All of my siblings, Tracy, Brandy and Ralph have a place in my heart that I could never express in words. I could not have a better support group. I knew they would never leave the battle until I did. What I didn't know was one of them would have to carry me out.

It would be impossible for me to choose one sibling over another. I couldn't. I am glad I never had to pick one to be my marrow match because they all have qualities I would be privileged to share. I feel grateful God chose for me. He must have been watching us for a while. He knew which one needed to be my donor; not just for compatibility reasons, but for their own resolution of self. God chose the one most would call the black sheep in the family to pull me off the battlefield. I'm glad he was watching Tracy as she faced these challenges. I'm glad he pulled her through, each time giving her one more small victory. I'm glad he heard her when she felt she had never accomplished anything worthwhile because she didn't have the paper to prove it. I'm glad, because in her race to come and be my big sister, he touched her life, gave her a vision, and made her my perfect marrow match.

She not only was given the chance to be the match but to be my anchor through this war. She may have given me marrow (she matched 6 out of 6 antigens), and platelets and cared for my son during my seven-week stay in the hospital, but deep down she gave me more than I ever expected.

Tracy, in her love and commitment, provided me the foundation of my faith in God to fight the war. She was much more than my bone marrow donor. She was to be my source of strength and insist that my faith would carry me through any battle, no matter how great. She continues to be my inspiration every day and I feel completely honored to be carrying a part of her in my body and soul.

I could continue with numerous accounts of my war with cancer. The health battles of continuous doctor visits, additional medical issues, rejection of transplants, and medications could make a book.

It is more important you see the boundless hope this military family uses to fight each battle. We have had tremendous support from military doctors, hospitals, community hospitals, schools, and the base community to make our battle a little less stressful.

It amazes me to think of what I have learned; that as an individual I can accomplish many things but as a "unit" we can accomplish whatever we put our minds to, no matter what the war may be.

I come from a long line of great servicemen and women and am proud they are a part of my heritage. I consider my mother and father to be a wonderful example of a true military couple. Neither wavered in their love and family commitment as my father proudly served his country for twenty-three years. They taught me, through their times of challenge and survival, that regardless of how small or great the battle, there will always be hope. My story of survival is dedicated to the two people to whom I owe my every hope, my parents, Retired Senior Master Sergeant Ralph E. and Joyce M. Piper.

Shawn Hall

Alphabet Soup

Husbands. They are the most "cussed and discussed" subject among married women the world over. Most of ours come/came packaged with a uniform and a service commitment, along with a few other semi-endearing idiosyncrasies.

But have you ever wondered what it is that makes them follow the military's siren cadence? Whether they are administrators, communicators, medics, engineers, aircrew members or whatever, they seem drawn to their service branches by some invisible uniting force. Is it patriotism? Adventure? Travel? Job Security? Lack of fashion imagination? All factors, perhaps. But the real common thread among military members is, I believe, something deeper. It came to me a while back as I overheard my husband's end of a phone conversation with a co-worker:

> "…Yeah, we got OSA support for our TDY to the JA/ATT conference. We're supposed to check in at the pax terminal at O-dark thirty and Then meet the DO at Base Ops at 0600 Zulu. ETD Scott is 1045. ETA Eglin 1115. There'll be a DV-5 and an O-6 enroute to SMOTECH on board, and a couple of JCS guys, so it'll be tight—no room for The Sticks…"

Say what? Then, woosh, there it was, in a flash so sudden that it rattled the laundry room dust off my MEd. Certificate.

Like ants to a picnic, these guys are drawn to the military life by some predisposing personality trait that makes them *dependent on abbreviated language.* Freud explained personalities whose fixations were oral, anal, and Oedipal, but he never even considered those who were alphabetical!

A well-designed and -conducted research project into this Language Abbreviation Fixation (LAF) could produce invaluable new insights into the uniformed personality, and might well be considered vital to our domestic sanity, if not national security. The Department of Defense (DoD) could cover this with a minor budget line titled Project "Dependency on Abbreviation among Military Members (DAMM).

There is no doubt in my mind that the DAMM data would reveal a disproportionate number of military types who demonstrated tendencies to LAF early on. As children, many were involved in secret clubs, which required passwords or phrases, such as "Shazam", or "Levram Niatpac" (Captain Marvel spelled backwards). A high percentage probably risked pre-adolescent annihilation from irate others whose cupboards were stuffed with boxes—minus tops of stale Cheerios, Sugar Pops, Corn Flakes, and Rice Krispies, mutilated to provide the POPs necessary to order Dick Tracy Super Decoder Rings or Star Cadets' Secret Language Dictionaries.

The LAF phenomenon is in no way confined to Air Force blue, or to any other single service. The Army's history, as well as the Coast Guard's and Marines', is rife with LAFers. As for the Navy, well, you have read Tom Clancy's books, haven't you? I rest my case.

Don't we really need to know the effects of LAFs on productivity in the workplace? Certainly LAFers are remarkably adept at managing their dependencies, operationally speaking. A case in point can be found in the multiservice Transportation Command (USTRANSCOM). In order to bridge the treacherous tide of alphabet soup swirling through their organization, the powers that be have elected to use *numbers* in job titles. Take the job of the DO (Director of Operations) at HQAMC. His USTRANSCOM counterpart is called the J-3 the "keep them airplanes rollin" guy at HQAMC is the LG. At USTRANSCOM that would be the J-4. However, at one time this job was filled by the J-3, making him the J-3/4, or would that be the J-7? Or would this individual be a fraction of one whole J? Well then, you see the problem!

Could this be the first sign of a companion dependency, perhaps Eccentric Number Use Fixation (ENUF)?

Thankfully, there is no current evidence that the apparently rampant rate of LAFable characteristics among military members occurs in the spousal ranks. We do not generally refer to our children as "dependent #1, 2 or 3…" We simply call our organization the OWC, without undue need to add a vowel to make it pronounceable. We do not characterize our social functions as "grip 'n grins." And I have never heard a single wife refer to the Scott OWC honorary president as the MINCAMC (Ma'am In Charge, HQAMC) or the WOCTRANS (Wife Of Chief, USTRANSCOM).

Without truly understanding the contagion issue, however, we must adopt a defensive posture in living with a LAFer as a mate. It is necessary of course to shop at the BX, renew our IDs at CBPO, survive TDYs, ORIs and remotes, enroll our children in DEERS and file TRICARE claims ASAP. We may also go through a coasting/withdrawal phase of FIGMO (Forget It, Got My Orders) when approaching a PCS. These things are part of living with a LAF.

But until we get some DAMM information to light our way, we must continue to cope in the dark with LAFing in our marriages. We *can* live with this condition, but it will require continuing vigilance and new knowledge. For if we do not come to understand the dynamics involved, the dependency could snowball. A LAF could become ENUF, and from there ladies, who can say? It could be the end of conversations, as we know it.

Maryellen Mills

Far Away From Home

I was thirty years old when they died. Living halfway across the country was the closest assignment we were able to get, and yet too far away to be of help. Too far away to do those things for dying parents that allow you to learn to cope and to accept terminal illnesses, if that is possible at all.

Humanitarian assignments were only granted for the active duty spouse and even then certain criteria must be met. I knew that. But now I was going to "feel" what that meant. Suffice it to say there is not enough paper or ink on the face of the earth to describe those feelings of helplessness, distance, isolation, frustration, resentment, anger and pure self-pity. I needed to be with my mother and eight months later with my father. It didn't happen. Was this lifestyle we chose a mistake?

Guarantees do not exist in any chosen profession or lifestyle. I still wish I could have been there even after all these years. With four small children and a husband whose mission was to end the cold war and train others, how could I actually leave my primary responsibilities and care indefinitely for ailing parents? I couldn't, nor was I meant to, although I didn't realize it at the time.

The grieving process took a long time for me personally, but eventually it did take place. Fortunately, today there is a lot more help available than in times past.

Twenty-one years later it was again time to make a very similar decision. But now retirement was closer than farther away! My in-laws were declining in health. As time went on it became apparent my husband's parents could no longer take care of themselves in a way they deserved. The decision became crystal clear. If they were willing, we would have them live with us, my husband would retire from active duty one year before we planned, and we would set forth on a "new" mission.

We began that process, but not without serious soul searching and some frank discussions with the folks. Such times are difficult for everyone, but mental attitude means everything. It was important to consider their needs, but not at a price to sacrifice our own needs as well. It took me more than six months to find an area that met most of the criteria that would make our cohabitation as comfortable as possible, and within our means.

Even with the best arrangements, the stress of retiring from the Air Force, the last child graduating from college, making our last move, and moving the folks from their home of thirty years into "their" space can have its toll.

I look back and think of my own parents, and I can now see the time would not have been right for us to take care of them. The circumstances would have become intolerable, given our situation at the time. And our family would experience other future crises requiring tremendous amounts of stamina and faith.

Little did I know another opportunity would present itself, and this time we would be better able to take on the responsibility and privilege of caring for elderly parents.

Replacing the Air Force "mission" with another type of mission has been gratifying because we believe we made the correct decision. Where are we now? Dad died a little over one month after he and Mom moved in, and only a few days after my husband retired. That was hard—and still is.

All those wonderful and caring military friends are still here for us, and for that we are grateful. A decision thirty years ago to say "yes" to the military lifestyle was good and right.

The next chapter in life has begun!

Barbara Sutherland

Fourteen Friends' Guide to Eldercaring

Years ago, whenever Air Force spouse Anne Roadman and her high school friends gathered together, their conversations centered around boyfriends, dating, children, careers etc. Gradually, as the years passed, those discussions began to gravitate toward the care of elderly family members.

Since graduation from high school in 1962, this group of fourteen women has held yearly reunions. The eight that live in the northern Virginia area also meet monthly. It was at one of these meetings that the group decided to write a book and share their thoughts and insights into care for the elderly.

Fourteen Friends' Guide to Eldercaring is different from most books on this subject. Not only do the authors state facts and give advice, they also share their personal experiences and challenges. It emphasizes the "care of the caregiver" and encourages them to journalize their thoughts and observations.

The book took about two years to complete. Once they started brainstorming, the project was well on its way. Anne says the most rewarding part for her has been "the positive feedback you get from those who have read the book, and knowing that you've helped them in some way."

Paulette K. Johnson

Stove Pilot

In 1948 the Maxwell Air Force Base Women's Club compiled a cookbook entitled Stove Pilot. *Initially it was a fundraiser for the Benefit of Overseas Relief. Since there were no computers, few typewriters and no Kinkos, the entire book was handwritten. Drawings and sketches accompanied most recipes. The club's efforts were enormous and their success quite impressive.*

Thirty-seven years later the Maxwell Officers' Wives' Club proudly reprinted the original version. Below is a portion of the "Foreword" from the 1985 edition.

Foreword

When this book was originally published in 1948, the Air Force was only one year old. Many of the contributors were still adjusting to peace time service. Maxwell was already established as the center of continuing education in the Air Force and many flying aces found themselves flying desks.

The ravages of the war in Europe prompted the spouses to collect clothing for the Overseas Recovery or Marshall Plan. The Women's Club of Maxwell had no trouble collecting clothes—there were over 1,700 active members—the problem came in paying the postage. The first month's postage was over $150.00, a sizable sum in 1948 dollars. Mrs. John Frisbee, organizer of the clothing drive, and Mrs. Edwin S. Chickering, president of the Women's Club, came upon the idea of a cookbook to raise funds to cover the postage costs.

All members and spouses were asked to contribute an original or family favorite recipe, handwritten, to Mrs. Dudley D. Hale. From over 1,000 recipes collected, Mrs. Harold W. Grant and Mrs. William H. Wise culled 300 of the best ranging from cocktails to desserts. The diversity is tremendous from Sips and Tidbits to Rabbit Food; the style and selection of recipes reflects the editor's concern for making the *Stove Pilot* a profitable venture. Three women, Mrs. John Driscoll, Mrs. Hunter Harris, and Mrs. Robert H. Fricke did the charming artwork often entwined with the handwriting.

Due to the aggressive sales campaign of Mrs. Grant, over 500,000 copies were sold between 1948 and the early 1960's. The Women's Club was able to help fund an orphanage near Dunkerque, France, equip a hospital operating room in a children's colony outside Milan, Italy, help provide books for the Free University in Berlin, as well as mailing clothing to England, Korea, and to Displaced Person's Camps in Europe. *The Stove Pilot* succeeded well beyond its original financial goal.

A Cruise to the Orient

I did not know a thing about large ships, yet, in November 1951, there I was in Seattle about to embark for Japan. All I did know was that it was the only way our small daughter and I were going to reach my husband.

When I was assigned a cabin on promenade deck with no cabin mate, I wondered why. I soon found out. It was the most forward cabin on ship, very small, and the bunks ran crossways of the cabin. I would soon learn the significance of that. It makes rough seas seem rougher!

We sailed at one o'clock in the afternoon from Seattle. Everyone was out on deck. All was calm and beautiful. There were no bands playing or crowds wishing us bon voyage. That would have been wonderful; but, more importantly we were at long last on our way.

Dinner at round tables with white linens, menus, and helpful mess stewards made us feel we were on a luxurious cruise. All that ended about eight o'clock in the evening when we hit the ground swells off the coast of Alaska. The ship began to roll and the passengers, mostly wives and kids, began to reel. We had all been so excited about our destination, we hadn't thought much about being seasick. No one can ever convince me that feeling seasick is all a state of mind. The little ones got sick—and they didn't know they were at sea!

The next couple of days were spent close to the cabin, but I knew we could not survive ten days of that. So, I managed to get Brita and myself up on the sundeck. A combination of fresh air, sunshine, and the fact that the captain had changed the route and dropped south, enabled us to gradually become better sailors.

Two days out of Yokohama, a terrible banging awakened me. Nearly everything in the cabin was metal and everything was moving. The worst was the top bunk ladder I had stored in the closet. I got up to secure it, but it was treacherous. By this time, the chair, heavy as it was, was sliding across the floor; the luggage, heavy as IT was, was traveling on its own. I thought of the baby's night bottle (glass only, in those days). It was on the shelf above the sink. Though there was a high rim around the shelf, it went off into the sink before I could reach it. One less bottle! I put the ladder at the back of the top bunk with a rolled blanket in front of it. I pushed the chair against the cabin wall (bulkhead) and tipped the suitcase on its side and put it tight against the chair. To show how well we had adjusted to shipboard life, I wasn't a bit ill, even though the ship felt like it was standing on end! And Brita did not even wake up!

The next morning our dining room steward was a bit pale, even green. He was not only amazed to see us at breakfast after such a bad storm, he was amazed how well WE looked!

Beverly Bogie

Winging It

"*Fred Astaire was justifiably admired for his grace and style in dancing. But someone pointed out that Ginger Rogers did everything he did—only backwards and in heels!*"

Author Unknown

"Space A"

The term "Space A" is short for Space Available. The military community uses it when referring to non-duty travel aboard military aircraft.[12] In most cases a family member must travel with their sponsor. In a few locations family members can travel without the active duty member. A closely monitored Environmental and Morale Leave (EML) program for family members is where the following story begins.

Guam: A tropical island paradise with beautiful beaches and fabulous weather, and only thirty-five miles long and five miles wide. "Island fever" can strike at any time! At the sign of the first symptom it is time to pack your "boonie" (short for boondocks) bag, sign up at the Air Passenger Terminal (then affectionately called MAC "T" by some) and head out on an Environmental and Morale Leave. It was on a return from an EML where I begin my story.

My friend Lori and I had traveled to Kadena Air Base in Okinawa from Guam for a little attitude adjustment and some shopping. That accomplished we signed-up for a return flight home. The Space "A" system in the 80s had greatly improved from the system that required travelers to be at roll call for every departing flight, or go to the bottom of the passenger list and

---

12 The number of Space A passengers on any flight is determined by its mission and AF regulations. Not all flights offer seats to Space A travelers.

start all over again. That was the 80s. Today, at the turn of the century and with a giant leap in technology, even that system had far to go.

Re-energized we were headed home to Guam. Since Guam was not the destination of many travelers we were quite certain we would not have a problem returning to our island in the Pacific. Tankers (KC-135s) flew from Kadena to Guam on a routine basis.

After being designated a seat (troop carrier kind), I called home to let my husband know I would be returning after midnight. He immediately told me that he would be flying a B-52 that night and the plane I was scheduled to take would be refueling it. How exciting to actually be on a plane and watch my husband refuel his aircraft!

We took off late at night and after a couple of hours rendezvoused with the BUFF (the nickname for the B-52). It was a dark, eerie night. Fortunately a full moon helped illuminate the sky.

After several hours of flying the crew asked if we would like to watch the refueling from the "boom"[13] pod. We had been secretly wondering when they would ask us. Lori and I quickly settled into our spaces on either side of the boom operator and watched him guide the boom to the area just above the window of the cockpit. Our adrenaline was pumping! Words cannot describe how ominous that B-52 looked as it pulled up under the KC-135. We could look right into the cockpit of this huge airplane flying only a few yards below.

We were just settling in and enjoying the experience when over my headset came the words "Break away. Emergency. Emergency." I immediately thought of my husband and the

---

13 The boom is the nozzle on the KC-135 that transfers fuel from the Tanker to another aircraft while in flight. It is controlled and operated from the back of the aircraft by a specially trained boom operator.

potentially dangerous situation he might be in. At the same time I knew he and the other crewmembers were well qualified to handle any emergency.

Lori began asking me questions and I confidently told her not to worry. I told her the crew of the B-52 is trained for all kinds of emergencies and would follow procedures and, I assured her, would land safely. It was then the boom operator looked at me and told me, "Ma'am it isn't the BUFF having the problem, it's OUR plane that declared the emergency." Lori told me later that after he said that, my eyes became as big as saucers.

We quickly left the boom pod and strapped into our seats, clutching our oxygen tanks to our bodies, neither one of us saying a word. My confidence in AF pilots and their training had quickly diminished now that I was the immediate beneficiary of a safe or not-so-safe landing. So much for all my accolades.

As you can surmise, the problem turned out to be a "minor emergency" (an oxymoron to me). We landed safely and without incident. Without question we were in very capable and very professional hands.

Which brings me to the moral of the story: Confidence is the feeling you have before you fully understand the situation.

Paulette K. Johnson

Top Ten Rules to Live by for Air Force Spouses

#10   Adopt the Policy, "Home Is Where the Air Force Sends You"

Some of the best assignments are in places like North Dakota, Alaska, and overseas. There is often more camaraderie and better friendships built in these places. Concentrate on the positive. It takes less energy and you are more productive.

#9   Bloom Where You Are Planted

Concentrate on the "now" and not the "when." That will take care of itself. Every place has some advantages over others. If you look you will find them. Find new talents. Watch them grow.

#8   Take Advantage of Surroundings

Too many people never take in the sights and opportunities of their locales. Spend weekends at the beach when you are stationed in Montgomery. Tour a national park when you are in Colorado. See the monuments in Washington, DC. Leave each place knowing all you can about it. The tour will fly by.

#7   Volunteer, Volunteer, Volunteer

Not only will it be appreciated, it will make you a part of the base and community faster than anything else. Leave knowing you made a difference.

#6 Participate/Socialize

Attend squadron and base events. You will meet people and cultivate friendships. Consider it an opportunity to do some "networking."

#5 Be Flexible

Some say it is the key to success. Some Air Force members say it is the key to Air Power. It most certainly is the key to adjusting to Air Force living.

#4 Take Care of Yourself

Make time for yourself. Even if it is only a few minutes a day or an hour or two a week. You and everyone around you will benefit from it.

#3 Take Care of Your Family

You will often be the only parent home to discipline, encourage, and love your children. This is never easy. Look for support. Call a friend. Stop in at the Family Support Center.

#2 Take Care of Your Spouse and Your Marriage

Make time to rekindle the fires and to have fun with your husband. Hire a baby-sitter occasionally. The children will survive, and even thrive. Be a couple. One day the job and the children will be gone. Have something to hold on to. Don't just co-exist.

#1 Keep a Sense of Humor

Laugh through the hard times; find humor in the trying times. It will keep your marriage, the Air Force, your children, and your soul in a better place.

Nancy Evans

Recipe For An Unforgettable Dinner

The first dinner my husband and I ever went to with Chinese dignitaries was truly memorable. The Foreign Affairs Bureau took the Air Force personnel to dinner at the world-renowned Peking Duck Restaurant.

I was seated between the Chinese general's wife and the interpreter. After we were seated, the waitress began to serve the meal. Seconds after she began to put little sauce dishes on the table, a cockroach appeared. He came out from behind one bowl and began walking over to my sauce bowl.

You have to understand that I'm not good with bugs. When I see a spider, my family has to run and kill it for me. So you can imagine my distress when he stood on his hind legs and starting sniffing at my bowl! Not finding anything he liked, he got down and started walking right toward me.

The Chinese general's wife was looking, so I tried to keep calm. I didn't want to make a scene by screaming, "Cockroach!" so I turned to the interpreter and politely said, "Excuse me, there's a bug on the table."

The interpreter went to get the waitress, but the cockroach was still coming at me, so I stood up. The waitress finally came, put her hand over it and took it away. Everyone was looking at me. I couldn't just stand there, but I couldn't just sit down either. I figured everyone would wonder what was wrong with me. Thinking quickly, I announced, "Excuse me. I'm going to the ladies' room." I thought I'd smoothed the problem over and the rest of the evening would be fine. Well, while I was in the ladies' room, I missed the presentation of the ducks.

I was a little disappointed, but since we were going to be in Beijing for two years, I thought I'd see the presentation another time. After I'd returned to my seat, the servers returned with the duck's head. It was split down the middle and cut open. The head was presented to the outgoing air attaché's wife and me. Then they handed me a pair of chopsticks. As their honored guest, they expected me to eat it.

I picked up my chopsticks and took a bite. I'm not sure what part I ate and I wasn't about to ask. I'm just glad ducks have small heads.

Carol Garrison

Honey, I've Got Orders

On 23 December 1943, with two children and another one on the way, he was drafted. There was no deferral. That was the beginning. I was alone with the children for more than seven of our first fifteen years together.

Since it was Christmas, we made quick arrangements to move near my parents. The small country house I found had no modern conveniences, so I moved in with a kerosene stove, a water bucket and chamber pots—all in the middle of an Iowa winter. I had never fired a heating stove before, so the first night I was alone with the children I filled it with coal, and turned the damper so it wouldn't heat up too much. Low and behold, the house filled with smoke. That was my first lesson—do not turn the damper too far. I never wanted anyone to know, but I had a good cry.

The next year I moved into the Methodist Parsonage. I renewed my teaching certificate and was able to substitute teach in the local school. My social life consisted of a game of cards in the evening with other teachers.

After two years Dean returned home. Eventually we bought an old house in Des Moines and Dean joined the Air National Guard. In 1951 his unit was called to active duty, and we were on the go again. After finishing the school year and renting our house, we journeyed to be with Dean in the Northeast. Home in Maine was a converted three bedroom barracks.

When we arrived, there was no furniture in what was to have been furnished quarters. A washing machine and double bed were all that we shipped. The children slept on army cots and office furniture decorated our living and dining areas. Eventually we got a stove and a refrigerator to replace the hot plate and cooler. A few second-hand pieces of furniture were added. However, living there wasn't a hardship. Our quarters were above the furnace room so it was warm, and we were all together. The skiing, tobogganing and fishing kept us all busy and I began my volunteer work at the Red Cross blood bank.

Word came that Dean's group would soon be leaving to open a new base in Louisiana. One evening my husband came home and said the packers would be at our place the next morning. With three children and the prospect of ten days of travel ahead, I started the washing machine and it ran until the packers had to take it!

The move had been hectic and kept us very busy. All at once I realized that no one had remembered my birthday. I baked a cake for supper and carried it into the dining area singing "Happy Birthday" to me. It was a surprise to everyone. Then Dean thought a moment and said, "This the 12th—your birthday was yesterday!" Now I was surprised!

Living in Louisiana was a wonderful introduction to Southern style living. We were able to enjoy summer activities in contrast to the winter sports we were used to. Once again I volunteered at the local Red Cross. A staff position became available and I was hired. Dean was so happy in the military that I encouraged him to make it a career. He was released from the Air National Guard, signed with the Air Force, and promptly received orders for a one-year tour in Saudi Arabia! The children and I moved into the servants' quarters of the chapter building. This solved many problems for me, as my car, phone, utilities and rent were provided. I was even able to hire help with housekeeping and cleaning.

When Dean returned a year later we headed to Carswell Air Force Base in Ft. Worth, Texas. Japan came next, then back to Carswell, north to the Pentagon and overseas to Germany.

Our last assignment was Seymour Johnson Air Force Base in North Carolina. One year later Dean retired with thirty-two years of military service.

We returned to our roots in Humeston, Iowa, and it was our home for the next seventeen years. By this time our parents had died and we had dropped off the children in different states. We enjoyed living in a big house where we could move walls, remodel, and make it a home we enjoyed sharing with our families. However, Dean and I knew that we would make one more move. This time it was to be with people we had lived and served with during our Air Force tours—The Air Force Enlisted Men's Widows Home.

When we left Iowa we packed an inflatable mattress, a card table, and four folding chairs into our motor home and started on our journey. Our neighbors in Iowa asked, "Do you mean to say you are moving into a house you have never seen?" They didn't realize that we had been doing that for thirty years!

For the last ten years we have lived in Florida and love being with people who have enjoyed the same type of life. Military living has taken us to all parts of the world. Along the way we made many important stops: Old Ironsides, Broadway in New York City, Ellis Island, Statue of Liberty, Smithsonian Institute, Monticello, Grand Canyon and Disneyland.

Our children have traveled all over the world and learned so much about other cultures. We've called many places home and have enjoyed them all. I tell them they don't know how lucky they are.

Kathlyeen Sponsler

The Air Force Enlisted Men's Widows and Dependents Home Foundation, Inc.

In the 70s a survey discovered thousands of widows, dependents of AF enlisted personnel, living in poverty. Low pay and frequent moves left many widows without the means to support themselves.

The AF Enlisted Men's Widows and Dependents Home Foundation, Inc. was tasked to help these AF families. They began with the purchase of 379 housing units at two Florida locations.

Teresa Village in Fort Walton Beach was purchased in 1975, and Bob Hope Village in Shalimar opened in 1985. An assisted living facility on forty-six acres next to Bob Hope Village is also underway.

Take Wing and Fly

This year, as my husband celebrates twenty-two years in service, I look back and wonder how much credit the Air Force deserves for my accomplishments, my joy with life, and my optimism about the future. The answer is simple: A lot. Of course, my husband deserves equal kudos, but one without the other might not have led to the totally delightful situation in which I find myself today.

I was in my late twenties when I married Don, and had spent the past two years working in Boeing's finance department—a fitting position for someone with a BA in Spanish and Political Science. I enjoyed the work, but when, a year later, Don was transferred, I was equally delighted to chuck it in order to move to New Mexico.

Before I tell you about my life in Albuquerque, I must backtrack and explain a small detail of our "pre-nup" agreement—you know what I mean, that on-going dialogue between two people who are considering sharing their lives. A major point of our discussions revolved around work.

First, while Don might have a limited amount of flexibility in career planning within the Air Force, there was an authority higher than our union that might, at any given time, derail or interrupt our wishes, plans, goals, and just life in general. In order for harmony to prevail, this lack of control over very basic life elements had to be accepted without outward complaint. (Inner grousing was allowed for limited periods.)

The second half of work discussions were in regards to my own employment. While I would have been tickled pink to eat chocolates and read books all day (employing, naturally, a cleaner and nanny to do the in-home chores; paid for, in case you're wondering, by Don's Air Force salary), that was neither practical nor, to be honest, a lifestyle that held more than a passing attraction. For his part, Don wanted to be married to someone who had her own interests beyond house and home. Therefore, we agreed that I would work, if only part time, out of the house.

Knowing that we would be stationed in Albuquerque less than two years, I did not attempt to find the kind of job I had left, i.e., one that is career oriented with a serious commitment involved. Not that my wants mattered, for I learned from military friends just how hard such positions were to come by. After all, what company wants to invest time and money in training someone who they know won't still be there in two or three years? If the job is designed for the long haul, a military spouse is not a wise investment.

Instead, I opted for self-employment. Combining my fabulous typing skills with one of the very first home computers off the assembly line, I opened a word processing business. Operating out of our home, I focused on the University of New Mexico as a client base, and spent the next sixteen months building the business. By the time we left Albuquerque, I turned a part-time typing job into a round-the-clock marathon. I was a success, but a tired one—not to mention frustrated with the prospect of starting all over again.

Our next stop was the Air Force Academy at Colorado Springs, where Don taught Physics. As we lived on the Academy, it would have made sense to focus my business on the cadet wing. (In those days, cadets didn't use computers, much less have two in every dorm room.) Don worried, though, that such employment might present a conflict of interest, particularly as I could never resist correcting grammar, punctuation, and sentence structure as I typed. Blocked from working locally and disillusioned by the logistics of typing for students twenty minutes away in Colorado Springs, I "dabbled" at re-starting my word processing business.

We had been at the Academy just five or six weeks when Don had to attend a meeting in Gunnison, a small town in the middle of a bunch of mountains in central Colorado. I accompanied him (a perk of self-employment), and was enjoying a quiet night with my husband in a cozy restaurant when he asked, "So what are you going to do about a job?"

So much for dabbling. I tried to steer the conversation away from anything that might be regarded as a firm promise to "look for work" by sighing over how I envied Don his career. As a young boy, he'd yearned to fly for the Air Force. When we met, he was a C-141 pilot. As a college student, he was attracted to the teaching profession. His current job at the Academy filled that square in spades.

What I was expressing was my envy of his ability to fulfill his dreams. Don surprised me by asking what my dream was. I was stunned, partly because I'd never put my dream into words, but mostly because it seemed such an impossibility that I'd never admitted it to myself.

When I told Don I wanted to be a writer, a novelist, both of us were amazed—Don understandably so because, in three years of marriage, I'd never so much as whispered such ambitions. But it shocked me too, if only because even in my wildest flights of fantasy, the closest I'd ever imagined coming to that career path was as a secretary to a prolific novelist.

That night, in the middle of a Colorado snowstorm, Don made the idea of pursuing a writing career seem feasible. All he'd ever wanted was for me to have a life of my own, and if it meant holing up with a computer for hours and days at a time, then there would never be a better opportunity for me to try it.

When children came along, I would be able to deal with their needs without compromising my own goals.

Getting a new job with each military move would no longer be an issue.

I'd be following my dream.

Reality dashed my hopes when Don said his only request was that we put a time limit on this endeavor. I about cried, only to listen in disbelief as he said, "If you don't publish within ten years, we should probably have this talk again."

Four years later, the first of many novels hit the stands under my pseudonym, Victoria Leigh. (Who can say Erbschloe, much less spell it?) A half-dozen military moves and one child later, I'm happy as a clam, spreading my wings from novels to ideas for screenplays and adaptations of stories I've already published. The wealth of travel and experience afforded my family by the Air Force has been a pivotal factor in my career, and there are days that I wonder if I would have taken the chance if this special opportunity had not been dangled in front of me by my husband's employer.

Vickie Erbschloe

Vickie Erbschloe is an award winning author under the pen names Victoria Leigh and Emma Jane Spenser.

Thelma and Louise in Italy

Here are some excerpts from several articles written by two spouses while their families were stationed in Italy. When they realized it was much better to enjoy their experience of living in a foreign land then complaining about it, they decided to "pen" their adventures for the benefit of all.

Living in Naples is full of inconsistencies: you have water, you don't—it's good water, it's bad water—you have electricity, you don't—you make it home from the base unscathed or you don't—your telephone works or it doesn't—the list is endless. The one consistent thing is the availability of good food and wine—lots of it!

Since all life in Naples begins at the four-lane highway, so will we. If you encounter peril as you are driving, remember to always honk your horn or flash your headlights continuously. All Italian drivers believe that anything you do while honking your horn or flashing your lights is sacred. Traffic can be heavy. If you can't pass the person in front of you, position your car within six to eight inches of his bumper and sit on your horn. Passing becomes possible when there is not a car to your *immediate* left.

With that advice behind you, it is time to hit the culinary road. Our first dining experience is Il Cerbero near the Parco Azzuro. If you value your life, park inside the gate and enter the restaurant from the waterside (around back). We highly recommend the Vino Rosso di Tavola (it was a very good week), especially after the first glasso. The linguine with crabmeat is very tasty if you must have food with your wine. Some English is spoken if that's important to you. Personally, we find our Italian improves with wine.

Another restaurant in this general area is the Giardino degli Aranci. To get to it you must travel over an ancient Roman road, which means you will constantly have your kidneys slammed against your pelvic bone. Slow down and watch for the Giardino degli Aranci sign. It has a small, obscure driveway with a large parking lot to the right. In good weather, eat out under the orange trees on the patio. We highly recommend the Vino Rosso di Tavola (it was a very good week) and we had more than one glasso. The canneloni is to die for and the grilled white fish as a secondo is hard to beat. The prices are very reasonable and not one word of English can be heard—try charades or have more wine.

For the more adventurous, head for the hard to find La Dragonara near Miseno. If you get lost, you write next month's column and tell us about your adventure. It is worth the extra effort to find because the food is terrific. If you don't like seafood, have the Vino Rosso di Tavola. It's almost as thick as the pasta. Enjoy a wonderful view and great seafood pasta. No English is spoken, but you will have a darling waiter. You wouldn't believe us if we tried to tell you a short cut home, so enjoy the adventure and figure it out yourself.

Our last recommendation is La Torre S'aracena near Monte di Procida. There will be whitecap parking (actually, you'll be lucky if he's wearing a hat at all). To make sure this is the right restaurant, see if it has mint green walls and fancy chairs with a little pink, green and blue geometric design on a cream background. There is a cute little waiter, who spent a month in San Diego learning English, so there is not a problemo. We highly recommend the Vino Rosso di Tavola— the penne with cream sauce and proscuitto was pretty good, too. If it's not the right restaurant, try it anyway and let us know how it was. Until next time…don't be afraid to get lost…you find the best restaurants that way.

Nancy Evans
Sharla Braunhardt

Assignment "Down Under"

One rainy morning shortly after our arrival in Australia, we headed to the card shop in Richmond where we lived. Adam, our son, was admiring all the colorful cards on the racks and the pictures of the many different types of animals unfamiliar to him. Adam was eager to learn about the animals unique to this continent.

While we were in the card shop a lady with an Aussie accent came over to say "hi" and to welcome us to her country. She could hear all the excitement in Adam's voice as he talked about the pictures and said she'd love to show him something. At this time, she reached underneath her sweater and brought out a possum. She explained that she worked for WIRES (Wildlife Information Rescue Service) and would gladly welcome us to her home to learn more about Australian wildlife.

What surprises we found when we visited her home! More possums and joeys than we could possibly touch. It was a delightful experience and a wonderful friendship was formed from that moment on.

Marie Sheraden

The Ultimate Sacrifice

"Freedom isn't free."

Author Unknown

Wings of Our Own

174

No Greater love

Betty McKaig met her future husband, a West Point cadet, at a party. They were married in the West Point Chapel on graduation day, 1927. John and Betty Lovell's life together began. What followed was a military life far from the norm. It ended in the ultimate sacrifice—having a husband declared missing in action.

The happy couple set sail to Hawaii for their first assignment. They spent one month on a ship, hardly seeing each other, because the men had to work. The women shared cabins apart from their husbands. When they arrived in Hawaii they found they were the lowest ranking new officers so they got the last pick of quarters. Betty had to deal with a coal range and flying cockroaches.

After several other assignments John received orders to Germany to the German General Staff School. To make it easier to learn the language John was sent to live with a German family, while Betty and the three children lived in Weimar. The Lovells would meet occasionally in a tavern to discuss family business.

The war was heating up in Germany. John was now assigned to the U.S. Embassy in Berlin. When things started to get worse he called his wife and told her to get out of Weimer immediately. She tried the airport, but all the planes were grounded. By then Germany had declared war and invaded Poland. Betty remembers standing by her garden gate, watching troops march by. It took five days before she could get a ticket to Berlin. She says, "Meanwhile, my husband had called and found out that I had left, so he and another officer went to the airport to meet us." There was a blackout in effect when they arrived. "I had one suitcase—because that's all I could carry—my dog in my pocket (a toy terrier), two boys hanging onto my coat, and I was carrying my little girl. With luggage everywhere and complete darkness, it was bedlam. I heard my name being called and zoned in on that."

The family lived in a rented apartment and was given old gas masks left from World War I, in case they needed them. It wasn't long after they arrived that the embassy ordered everyone to Denmark. "We were put aboard a train," Betty explains, "and were met at the border and assigned hotels." She continues, "We stayed there until John, who was working in Copenhagen, got word to me that I ought to go to a warmer climate. That meant to get out of there! Soon after, the Germans invaded Denmark. I was very fortunate to get on the ferry because the next day they stopped running."

Next, Betty and the children traveled to Florence, Italy, and were all set to leave for France when her husband begged her to go to Genoa, Italy—which she did. Eventually, she and the children were put on an evacuation list from Italy back to the states. Before they left however, Italy went to war against the Allies and she and her children endured five nights of bombing by the British.

Once the ship was in dock they were able to escape their harrowing ordeal. "I could see the American flag flying on the ship," she said. "It was hit with an anti-aircraft shell, but not severely damaged, so we were able to leave. When we got to Gibraltar, we didn't know if they'd let us through or not, but they flagged us on."

By 1940 the family was finally safe back in the U.S. Betty chose to live in Westminster, Maryland, a short distance from Washington, D.C., where she could get information on her husband's whereabouts. He stayed in Berlin as an attaché, inspecting prisoner of war camps.

When the United States declared war against the Japanese in 1941, the Germans interned all Americans staying at the Hotel Baden Nauheim. That group included John. He was freed in 1942, reunited with his family in the states, and assigned to the Pentagon. The Lovells were finally able to enjoy a normal, quiet life. Betty started volunteering at Children's Hospital, working with diabetics, burn cases, and polio victims. The hospital desperately needed her because most of the nurses had gone to support the war effort.

In 1946, John was offered an attaché position in Romania. Betty put their two boys in prep school and she and their daughter joined him. She became friends with Queen Helen and they did volunteer work together, but when the communists took over, the Queen mother and her son were forced to abdicate. The Lovells were granted permission to leave and went back to Washington, D.C., and John transferred to the newly formed Air Force.

On Thanksgiving Day 1950, he was sent on a special mission to Korea. A few weeks later, on December 4th, Betty received a telegram stating her husband had been shot down over Korea and was missing. No trace was ever found of the plane or the people aboard. Four years later, Colonel John Lovell was declared dead.

With very little pension and insurance, and three children in college, Betty was forced to find a job. She was lucky and found a job as an intelligence research analyst with the National Security Agency at Fort Meade, Maryland. She worked there for fifteen years, getting promoted along the way. In 1971, Betty moved to Air Force Village and has accumulated over 2,500 volunteer hours.

The Lovell family has not forgotten the circumstances surrounding their husband and father's death. Through documentation they have learned that there were three planes that left Japan on that fateful special intelligence mission. "Once they hit the coastline of Korea," Betty explains, "there was no more communication, so they have no way of really knowing what happened to the planes."

The Lovell family is committed to the pursuit of accurately accounting for all the MIAs in Korea. Betty says, "There are 8,000 people still on the MIA list. I went to a luncheon last year (1993) in Washington called 'No Greater Love.' A woman there got my name and said that she was the daughter of the pilot of the plane that my husband was on. Her father was taken off in a car so we know he was alive, but we never had any further information on my husband. We're now finding that the Russians held the men for interrogation."

Looking back on her life spent dodging the war zones of Europe, Betty says she wonders how she didn't have a nervous breakdown. "When you have three children alone in war zones, you were so afraid something might happen to you and what would happen to the children? You had to keep a front, see. Never let them know fear. I've always been matter of fact with the children, and they weren't disillusioned. They knew how to face life."

Betty's life experiences were far from ordinary and resulted in the ultimate sacrifice. How did she handle all the tough times? "I can only say that I can't imagine people not having some faith because if you didn't have some faith in a living God," she admits, "I don't know how you'd stand up to all the misfortunes or tragedies you have in life. I don't go out preaching, I just live it."

Sandra Troeber

Women in World War II

"Women had so many roles in World War II, from serving on the front line as nurses to taking the place of men on the assembly lines. They were also the wives and sweethearts of the fighting men, and in that role they were the moral support back home and the reason many men said they were so determined to stay alive."

Tom Brokaw
The Greatest Generation

The Story of "TAPS"

The Tragedy Assistance Program for Survivors (TAPS) is a national non-profit organization made up of, and providing a variety of support services to, all those who have faced the loss of a loved one in the line of military duty.

Bonnie Carroll, an Army Spouse, founded TAPS in the wake of a military tragedy—the deaths of eight soldiers, including her husband, aboard an Army National Guard aircraft in November 1992. In the months and years following the loss of their loved ones, the survivors turned to various grief support organizations for comfort; but when they turned to each other for comfort and to share common fears and problems, they found strength and truly began to heal. They realized that the tragedy they shared, losing a loved one in the line of military duty, was far different from other types of losses. They shared pride in their spouses' service to America, and tremendous sadness at the ultimate sacrifice their loved ones made.

On the next several pages are two very moving stories, written by Air Force spouses. They appeared in the TAPS newsletter.

A Place in My Heart

August 1990, my life seemed perfect. I had come a long way since 1979 when my husband had decided to leave the Air Force and to move to Birmingham, Alabama. The adjustments of civilian life had not been easy for me, but at last, all of the puzzle pieces were coming together. My son, Jeff, was a freshman in college, and my daughter, Kim, was completing her senior year of high school. My husband, Steve, and I both had rewarding jobs, and I had gone back to college to finish the degree I had begun twenty-three years before. We had a new house, and Steve was pursuing one of his greatest passions: flying RF-4s for the Air National Guard. I repeatedly asked myself how anyone could be so happy. I quickly found out it was not to last.

"There's a mad man in Iraq," I remember Steve saying. "He's invading the tiny country of Kuwait—killing, raping, and burning everyone and everything in his way. Someone's got to stop him. The unit's been asked to send volunteers to the Persian Gulf, and, Cyn, I've said I'll go." I felt the tears well up inside of me and then I pleaded with him not to go. He had already been to Southeast Asia for almost two years during the Vietnam conflict and in my mind, he had "filled the square" to risk his life. But Steve was focusing on his mission in the Air National Guard and he saw the need to rid a defenseless country of the dragon that was consuming it.

On October 8, my Steve was killed during a training flight over the deserts of Saudi Arabia. Both he and the pilot were killed instantly, although Steve had pulled the ejection handle to try to save their lives. They had been on a low altitude flight and the plane was at an angle that made survival impossible.

When they came to my office to tell me—the base commander, the personnel officer, and the wing commander's wife—

I felt an all-consuming numbness. Going to the airport to meet his flight home was the hardest thing I have ever done. Instead of being able to run to him, put my arms around him, and welcome him home as I had done so many times before, this time I waited in the shadows as the Delta luggage cart brought that cold, flag-draped metal box to the hearse. As I threw myself over the box, I heard someone saying, "I'm here, Steve. I'm here. I want to take you home, but they won't let me." I then realized that the voice was my own.

During the next three weeks, I lived in a black hole. I kept waiting and watching for him to open the door of the house and tuck his cap into the zippered pocket at the bottom of his flight suit as he always had. My imagination took over and became my reality. In my mind, he was really being held as a prisoner of war and the government did not want me to know because it might endanger his life. Other times, I thought that he was on a secret mission and that as soon as the war was over, he would come home. Odd, huh, how denial masks the intense pain that you feel?

The days grew into months and the months have now grown into years. Death creates a deep wound in our heart, and like a physical wound, it bleeds and makes us think that we too will die. I used to think to myself, "How can you hurt this intensely and still draw breath?" The emotional pain was quite often a physical pain in my chest. I finally knew what "heartache" was because my heart literally hurt.

The old adage that time will make it better is a great lie. The emptiness, the longing to have that one person back will never go away. Time makes the wound become a scar and, although the scar is a reminder of what we once had, we can now live with it.

I have to admit that during those first months I was not the best mother in the world. I was so consumed with my own selfish grief and with trying to survive that I often times neglected to realize that my kids were hurting just as deeply. We said things to each other that were hurtful and our relationships became strained.

Fortunately, our love for each other helped us to forgive. It was with the love and support of my family and of friends at church, at work, and the Air National Guard that the recovery process has taken place. I have never understood why Steve had to die. I have never understood, either, why my twenty-three-year-old daughter, Kim, had to die in 1996. But I have a very strong faith in a God who knows what the big picture is for my life, and He continues to bless me by introducing me to more caring friends. In fact, this article was written because my new friend, Bonnie, asked me to share a bit of my life with you. Over the years, people have told me I am strong. I do not consider myself to be strong, I consider myself to be a survivor. I chose to survive the sorrow and the emptiness.

I still cry for Steve and Kim, but I choose to do so in private. I want no pity, just understanding. I want to be someone about whom others who have lost a husband or child can say, "She's made it. So can I."

There are no promises that recovery is easy, just the assurances that there are people who want to help. Eight years ago, there was no organized assistance or support. The Air Force sent a casualty officer to tell me about Steve's life insurance, the educational benefits that were available, Champus, and survivor's benefits. It was, however, overwhelming at the time and there was no one who had "been there" to offer advice or support for the emotional turmoil I was experiencing. Today, TAPS exists as a group of your peers to fill this role. Because they understand, they respond immediately when a military spouse dies to offer comfort and assistance to survivors in so many ways.

In conclusion, as I have done so many times in the past, I thank you from the bottom of my heart for all of your prayers and your support; for your hugs and your tears, and for the compassion and comfort you have extended to my family and me these last eight years.

Cynthia Schramm

Precious Moments

I have not seen Patrick for four months. That is longer than we have ever been apart in the seven and a half years we were together. This time apart from him seems like an eternity for me. To think that I have to spend the rest of my days here without seeing his wonderful smile, hearing his charismatic rendition of *Oklahoma*, or feeling the warmth of a spontaneous dance in the kitchen is unbearable. I know that nothing can change what has happened. Patrick's body is dead and I miss it so much, but his spirit is living on in all of the lives that he touched.

Since his death I have received many cards and a few letters. The letters are what mean the most to me. It is like peeking into a part of his life that I was never able to share. I thought I knew all that there was to know about this amazing man. Friends tell me about how Patrick was in high school or in college before we met. They tell me memories of times they spent fishing with him or hanging out at the squadron bar. They share with me how they thought we were such a great couple and fun to be around. Patrick's college roommate told me that Patrick said, "That is the girl I am going to marry," after the first time he saw me. I never knew that.

These letters help me know that others thought he was as special as I did. I want to continue to learn all that I can about him. I want to talk about him. It keeps him alive for me as well as others. My love continues to grow for him even though I cannot see him. I appreciate all the small things that I took for granted before. I am very lucky to have such a great love in my life.

I know that Patrick is around me now. I know that he wants me to be happy and he is trying very hard to give me the strength to go on. I know that it is just his body that is gone, but that cannot belittle what his body meant to me. It gave me warmth, comfort, and a shoulder to cry on (which is what I need most right now). This is what I struggle with each day—the loss of his body and faith that his spirit surrounds me.

I buried Patrick's body one month after his F-16 crashed. I did not see the crash site or any evidence that he was really gone. I received a small box of his cremated remains. I imagined many different things. Perhaps he signed some secret paper that said he had to go under cover for years and leave his life behind. Maybe it is not his body in this box. I was reaching for anything to not believe that my 170-pound husband could be reduced to this. How could I believe that what these men had told me was true? The only proof that I had was that he did not come home.

It is so important for me to get all the available information about his crash and about his remains. I received the report about his accident last week, along with patches he was wearing during the crash. It did provide some answers for me, but also left me with many questions. I need to know what was left of his body. That is the part that everyone seems to want to shield from me. The "fragile widow" is the impression that I get. It is true my emotions are fragile, but I still need to know. I have an appointment with the head of the mortuary this week to discuss what was left of his precious body. I hope that it will provide me with the information I need to put my imagination to rest. I hope it will help me accept that I will not see him walking through my door again.

Getting involved with TAPS has helped me tremendously. After Pat's accident I reached for anyone to tell me what it is like to be a widow. How am I going to survive? How did you survive? TAPS has shown me women to admire and respect. I think of them on the days when I don't even want to get out of bed and face another day. They give me hope that I can survive.

Robin Potter

Kids Camp

Every year the TAPS organization hosts a Kids Camp for military children who have lost a parent in the armed forces. It is designed to help those children experiencing difficulty in dealing with the death of a parent or sibling. During this time of sharing and healing they bond with other kids who face similar losses.

Knowledge of Sacrifices Must Be Passed Down

I had begun to think that most Americans viewed Memorial Day as merely a three-day weekend that kicks off the summer season.

Indeed, the first question in my own mind usually centers on what my family might do to celebrate the extra day off. Should we attend a parade or backyard barbecue? Or should we perhaps go away for the weekend? Certainly, I know what the holiday is all about. After all, I come from a military family.

This past Memorial Day weekend, when my children had an extra day off from school, one of them asked, "What for?" This led to a discussion about Memorial Day.

My seven-year-old son was supposed to decorate gravesites with his Cub Scout Troop at Fort Rosecrans National Cemetery near San Diego. I thought the event would provide the perfect opportunity to really show the kids what it's all about.

My children know that both of their grandfathers served in the Air Force and their aunt is in the Navy—and, of course, they know very well the life of an Air Force "brat." But how do we bring home the importance of holidays like Memorial Day? The simple act of decorating the graves of those willing to die for our country and our freedom proved a wonderful and meaningful way to start.

On May 5, 1868, in General Order No. 11, General John Logan proclaimed May 30 a day to honor veterans. "The 30th day of May, 1868, is designated for the purpose of strewing with flowers or otherwise decorating the graves of comrades who died in defense of their country during the late rebellion, and whose bodies now lie in almost every city, village, and hamlet churchyard in the land," he wrote. The general would be pleased with the way his order is carried out today at national cemeteries around the country.

My family awakened before sunrise Saturday, May 29, and headed out to Point Loma, California, where the cemetery is located. Fort Rosecrans National Cemetery overlooks the city and offers a breathtaking view of the ocean. It is a peaceful place. We arrived early and were able to park nearby, but cars eventually lined the street for at least a mile.

Though decorating the 55,000 graves was sponsored by the Boy Scouts, those who turned out ranged from Scouts and their families to volunteers who had heard about the decorating through friends or family. Even with thousands of people in attendance, a peaceful silence fell like a blanket over the crowd as "Taps" was played and the colors retired.

Fort Rosecrans program assistant Delia Fernandez said it took the more than 1,500 volunteers only 45 minutes to decorate the 55,000 gravesites. "We just couldn't have done it without the help of the volunteers," she said. "We had Boy Scouts, Cub Scouts, Girl Scouts, Brownies, Campfire Boys and Girls—not to mention their families and other volunteers."

Some things never change. Although Logan's words were intended for those who died in the Civil War, they apply today. "Let us…gather around their sacred remains…let us raise above them the dear old flag they saved from dishonor." And so we did—the children took great delight in their job, even stopping occasionally to see whose grave they were honoring.

Too often these days I find myself shaking my head in disbelief as the troubling news of the day unfolds. It was heartening to see that so many people do know and care. Our veterans, active-duty men and women, and their family members have made—and will continue to make—many sacrifices for our way of life. The whole experience has brought to the forefront of my mind the importance of appreciation for our freedoms and for those who protect them—and the importance of passing it down through the generations. My family will take part in the Fort Rosecrans ceremony again next year.

As my family walked around, I heard one little boy ask his father, "Dad, are any of these people buried here heroes?"

"Yes," he answered. "Everyone here is a hero in one way or another."

Leslie Smith
Air Force Times
Reprinted with permission

...A Memorial Day Wish Comes True

A Stoneham, Massachusetts family's 15-year quest to have a soldier honored as the first to die in Vietnam ended Monday on Memorial Day.

At the Vietnam Veterans Memorial, as people streamed past the wall, Eunice Fitzgibbon placed flowers by the name of her husband, Air Force Technical Sergeant Richard Fitzgibbon, Jr. for the very first time. She also placed flowers by the name of her son, Richard Fitzgibbon III, who died in Vietnam in 1965.

The name of Fitzgibbon Jr., was not included when the memorial opened in 1982 because he died in 1956. The Department of Defense previously recognized the start of the conflict as 1961 but changed that date to 1955 after investigating Fitzgibbon's death.

Andrea Tortora
© 1999, *USA TODAY*
Reprinted with permission

Life in the Air Force

"Home is where the Air Force sends you."
Author Unknown

Home is Where the What Is?

In my years as an Air Force wife, I've discovered that some words in the English language do not have the same meaning to me as they do to many of my civilian friends. Take the word "home" for example. To a civilian, home means the place she or he lives. It's a house where the activities of everyday living are carried on. It's a place where the occupants watch the annual rising of the tulips planted five years ago. And somewhere inside that house there are marks on a wall indicating how much the children have grown. Within walking distance is another family called grandparents.

To a service family, home means something entirely different. Actually, home has two meanings within the Air Force, and it's not difficult to tell the difference when the word is used in a sentence. For example, a friend wrote a letter saying, "We went home for Christmas." And that "home" meant a small town in Kansas. It's similar to the civilian "home," but going home meant family reunions and in-laws and brothers and sisters. And it meant seeing a year-old granddaughter for the first time.

But the Air Force family uses "home" in another sense—unlike any other. Home is base housing, impossible to decorate. It's a TLQ. It's a tract house in a part of the state no one else would choose to live in. It's a trailer in Alabama; it's a dream house on the East Coast completed six months before the orders come for the West Coast. Home takes on a meaning not even inferred in Webster's dictionary. Let me explain by telling you a little about the homes my family has shared. Some of these memories may spark memories of your own.

Our first home was a furnished one-bedroom apartment in South Georgia. "Furnished" meant draperies and tablecloths and beautiful rugs. Some of the furniture were genuine antiques, and we had a view of a garden where poinsettias grew wild.

We shipped our few household goods to our next base and enroute spent three months in another "furnished" apartment in Oklahoma. The interior decorator had $300 to furnish three rooms and still had $100 left over when he was done. The personal possessions we had carried with us fit in the back seat of an Austin-Healey. Those months in Oklahoma were austere.

We had a view of a Japanese garden in Tacoma. In Seattle we saw Mount Rainier and Elliott Bay from our balcony. In Dover we got our first taste of base housing. I planted a dozen chrysanthemums there. For all the bad press on base housing, it's nice to know it's not my responsibility to fix the broken dishwasher or the stopped-up drain when my husband is on a trip. I'll gladly cut the grass for that little peace of mind.

In Charleston our base house overlooked the golf course. The floors were polished parquet. I had purchased a hammock to hang in the pines just before we got orders for Ohio. We rented a house there. The shingles were falling off, and the garage door never shut tight. Grass never grew on the lawn. But in my mind I'll always remember the glow in that house the Sunday morning we brought our son home from the hospital. In two months we again celebrated—graduation from AFIT and leaving that house.

At last, we owned our first house. A house with fruit trees and a fenced-in yard for a wandering child and a freedom-loving dog. We planted a garden and taught our son to swim in the pool. We painted. We paneled and carpeted the family room. We planted rose bushes and our very own tulips. And then, you guessed it, orders.

For those of you who like statistics, we have moved thirteen times. Four of those times, we moved ourselves. We have lived in three base houses, four civilian houses, a few apartments, other abodes, and once a trailer. Once was enough.

If you've had the luck to spend a TDY in Montgomery, Alabama, you must be familiar with Muddy Meadows. We didn't live there; we lived in Eagles' Nest. I was dumb enough to think we were on the right side of the tracks—until the rains came. They didn't call it Eagles' Nest because it was on high ground; it was called Eagles' Nest because it was owned by four bird colonels! When it did rain, our neighbors parked their Jeep between our two trailers, and by walking through the Jeep we could visit back and forth without getting our feet wet. I'll let you guess how deep the water was and how close the trailers were. My six-foot-two-inch husband had his leg in a cast that summer, and he'll never win any prizes for being a patient patient.

There was a period of eighteen months when we didn't even share the same quarters. I watched my sunsets over Elliott Bay while my husband described the beaches of Florida and the deserts of New Mexico in his letters. And then his letters told of jungles and a roommate I never met. He had a maid who didn't speak English. And it was the longest wait of our lives.

You may think I've been talking about houses. If that were true, I couldn't say we've had a home for the last fifteen years. Oh, yes—we've always had a home. Every one of those houses, apartments, motels, trailer, transient quarters and friend's spare bedroom was home. Because home is always where my husband hangs up his slacks and blue shirt. It is where my son sets down his "blankies" and favorite bunny. It is where I take out my sewing for just a few more stitches. Home is where we spend the night together before moving on one more time.

Margaret Baroniak
McGuire OWC Flair, March 1982

Moonlight and Roses

Mrs. Mildred Stearley symbolizes the officer's wife of the past: elegant and gracious. She looked very beautiful with her gray hair neatly set and her make-up on. She was wearing a pretty patterned dress.

As we began our interview, I couldn't help but notice the large oil painting of her husband Ralph, hanging on the wall behind her. The portrait of the handsome, two-star general in uniform made it seem like he was there, listening to our conversation.

Looking around the room, I noticed a silver tea set on a beautiful table right below the painting in the dining room. Also on the wall was a drawing of their favorite horse named Stoney Ford—a beautiful thoroughbred polo pony. Every item in the apartment was perfectly arranged including the elegant Oriental furniture. It was easy to imagine this couple in their younger days, entertaining their guests. It was the perfect setting to hear the story of her life.

At the time of this interview Mildred Stearley was eighty-eight years old and had been a widow for twenty-one years. She had been raised in the military and one of her father's assignments took them to the Philippines. It was there that she met Ralph. As was customary, a dinner party (a *despadeda*) was held to welcome the new arrivals and to bid farewell to those returning to the states. Ralph was Mildred's dinner partner that night. They soon became good friends. Ralph had learned polo during his days in the cavalry and he taught Mildred how to ride. One of their favorite Sunday outings was riding horses on the beach.

While in the Philippines, Mildred was asked to teach fourth and fifth grade at a school in Baguio. She remembers teaching the twenty girls and boys as a great experience. Ralph made weekend trips to see her. On one of those weekends, he proposed to Mildred. They were driving to a party on a rainy night and he pulled over on the side of the road to ask the question. She said yes, but wanted to wait until they were back in the states. "I wanted to be sure it was not just a moonlight and roses deal!"

One year later, Mildred's father was reassigned to the states and the family moved. Another year passed and sure enough, Ralph remembered Mildred's answer to his proposal and now was able to propose again. They were married on September 19, 1931, in Washington, D.C.

Ralph was a graduate of West Point, went into the cavalry, then transferred to the Army Air Corps in 1923. The Stearleys' bumpy military career took off from there. Although Mildred wasn't able to be with Ralph on every assignment, they did enjoy many duty stations together. They were living in Washington, D.C. when World War II kicked in. Mildred got involved in the Army emergency relief activities through the Woman's Club.

Then Ralph was assigned to command the 1st Tactical Division in North Carolina. They were told it would be temporary, so they lived in a hotel—for a year! The entire division then relocated to Shreveport, Louisiana. They moved into their quarters, and just when everything was in place, orders came for Ralph to go overseas. The furniture went into storage and back they went to Washington, D.C. Mildred was able to stay with her parents until she could find an apartment, and Ralph went off to fight the war. During that time her mother died of a heart attack. It was an awful shock for Mildred.

After getting her father used to life without his wife, Mildred joined the Red Cross as a volunteer. "I had taken a course as a staff assistant," she says. "I helped with taking histories of the patients when they came in, sort of doing personnel work." She did this six days a week and found being able to help others was very worthwhile.

After the war, Ralph stayed in the European theater to help write the history of the war. It was peacetime when Ralph finally returned. Mildred continued her work with the Woman's Club and also taught children's horseback riding classes. She had sixty students and held classes three times a week. "That was fun," she said. "I thoroughly enjoyed it and the children loved it."

Life was finally settling down for a little while, and the Stearleys were planning some much deserved leave, when Ralph got an unexpected call from Air Force Chief of Staff General Hoyt Vandenberg asking Ralph to meet him in Washington the next morning. Mildred recalls, "He looked at me and said, 'I'm afraid we're not going to get to take any leave. This sounds like I'm going to have to go over to the Pacific.' Sure enough, he called me that night and said his guess was right." Gen. Vandenberg had asked Ralph to take command of 20th Air Force in Okinawa.

It was a quick move. They learned of Ralph's assignment on Friday and were scheduled to leave Monday morning. Mildred remembers, "I spent that whole night labeling furniture for storage, permanent and intermediate, in case we could have some sent, but it turned out we could only take what the plane would hold." They were able to leave whatever they couldn't finish in the hands of good friends, and Mildred admits, "If it hadn't been for our friends, I don't know what we would have done."

Okinawa was a busy place during the Korean War. Mildred explains, "Ralph's job was sending bombers out from Kadena. General Vanderberg said my role was to be there in case some of the planes didn't get back. It would help with the wives who would be distraught." Mrs. Stearley's role was very important. It was understood that a senior officer's wife was more seasoned and could help the younger wives.

Mildred describes some of the other activities on the island. "Our Woman's Club kept busy all the time, making cookies for the men when they came back from their engagement or baby things for the native babies. We also helped the native women's club organize and they got to be very business-like about it all. It was really amazing. They wanted to learn about American ways and we'd have meetings in our home." Another contribution of the Woman's Club was helping set up a public health nurse program.

To offer aid to the natives, every unit on the island adopted a group of people. "Ours was the Deaf, Dumb and Blind children. They didn't have running water. We asked the construction company there if they'd tell us what to get and where to get it and how to go about arranging for it. Bless their hearts, they provided the material. The workers contributed their labor after hours and we raised money by giving bake sales and auctions. They were so generous about helping. It was really wonderful to see how much people tried to help."

In addition to all this work, Mildred was the Air Force representative of the Red Cross Gray Ladies. It involved coordinating and recruiting and assigning volunteers.

The Stearleys spent two and a half years on Okinawa, and then retired to Indiana. When General Stearley suffered a stroke in 1968, Mildred gave up her outside activities and focused entirely on her husband. "We probably had the five happiest years of our lives," she says fondly. "We did just what we wanted, when we wanted." Ralph Stearley passed away in 1973, five years after his stroke. The two had been happily married nearly forty-two years.

Mildred moved to AF Village because that's where Ralph wanted her to live after he was gone and could no longer provide for her. She keeps busy with her friends and various activities at the Village.

Her philosophy is to do the best you can at all times and look on the bright side. "It's the only way to live," she says. Every day she can gaze at her husband's picture realizing that her days of moonlight and roses did last a lifetime!

Sandra Troeber

DITY or Not to DITY [14]

We had been stationed at McChord AFB in Tacoma, Washington, for twelve years when one April afternoon my husband, with much trepidation, informed me that we had orders. I had lived in the same place my whole life.

After a two-week crying jag, my natural optimism took over and I decided to make the most of the situation. We were going to do a "Do IT Yourself" or a DITY move: you move all of your household goods yourself and the military reimburses you for the actual moving expenses and an additional one third of what they saved by not having a professional mover do it. I had a few very wonderful friends advise me against this course of action. One of these wonderful friends was my husband, but I had made up my mind. I was obsessed with saving money. I felt if I planned every detail, nothing could go wrong. Easier said than done. Here are the lessons I learned:

  * When you decide to clean your own house, if the stove alone takes more than eight hours to clean, you're in trouble.

  * Make sure you have a neighbor who is a loadmaster and is willing to help load the moving truck. Also, take advantage of large families, friends, passing football teams and every able-bodied individual to help you load. Feed them or they get cranky.

14 Air Force acronym for a Do IT Yourself move. *Ed.*

🕊 If your husband leaves after you because you have to get the kids to a fishing tournament in Spokane, and he still needs to weigh the truck, make sure he has a copy of the computerized itinerary and map that you spent so much time on. This oversight may result in him almost running out of gas in the middle of nowhere and having to buy four gallons of diesel fuel from a reluctant farmer.

🕊 An 18,000 pound moving truck towing a Ford Bronco will only go fifteen miles per hour over all four mountain passes between Tacoma and Grand Forks.

🕊 When you stay in a hotel, don't park the moving truck in the adjacent shopping mall parking lot. The mall may be resurfacing the lot the next morning.

🕊 Always keep the keys to the moving truck with the person who has access to the truck. Problems may occur if the person who has the keys is off purchasing sandals for his wife because her feet are so swollen she can't fit into her shoes, and the parking lot is waiting to be resurfaced. The possibility of watching all of your worldly possessions being towed away is not conducive to good mental health.

🕊 Make sure you have trained your children to like a variety of music or you will listen to the same two CDs for 1,400 miles.

🕊 Confirm that there really is "no waiting" on the base housing list.

It is imperative to know many able-bodied individuals who will be waiting breathlessly to help you unload your moving truck at your new house. If this in not the case, you and your husband will unload 9,000 pounds of household goods by yourselves. This does not optimize your back condition or marital happiness.

We did make it to Grand Forks AFB, got a house right away and almost everything made it in one piece. We also made some money on our move, which just about covered all our cold weather gear and winterized our vehicles.

Teri Chlanda

This article first appeared in Off-Duty Magazine *in the November-December 1998 issue.*

Yes Kristen, There is a Santa Claus...

However in Oklahoma
He drives a team of Armadillos...

I was born and raised in Fairborn, Ohio. I am sure a lot of you are saying, "What does that have to do with Christmas?" For those who question, a lot! In Ohio, it gets cold at Christmas time, there is snow on the ground, and there are fireplaces. I grew up believing in the traditional Christmas story...Santa wears a red furry suit, drives a sleigh that lands in the snow, comes down a chimney, and everyone knew that the real Santa Claus was at Rike's, a large department store in Dayton, and the rest were merely his helpers...then, I grew up, married my husband (not necessarily in that order!) and had a child of my own. I soon found myself in places where the "traditional" Christmas story could not be told and be expected to be believed.

I first started lying about Christmas in South Carolina. No snow, no fireplace. I told our daughter, Kristen, that Santa comes in a radio flyer wagon powered by eight palmetto bugs (we all know that they are really roaches). We tied up the dog so Santa could gain access through the front door! She believed me.

Then we were stationed in Arizona. Arizona is bizarre! They make snowmen out of tumbleweed. In downtown Chandler, they construct a huge Christmas tree from tumbleweed, chicken wire, and lights. In Arizona, Santa wore jogging shorts and a tee shirt, and drove a four-wheel drive vehicle. Instead of leaving him cookies and milk, we left him some salt tablets and sun tea. Kristen believed me.

Travis AFB, California, was our next stop. There, Santa wore a red and white sweat suit with green striped Adidas. He drove a Mercedes with one of those California personalized plates, HO3. His snack was wine, crackers and cheese. (Halfway through the Holly Hobby playhouse, Santa really appreciated the snack). Kristen believed me.

Now, we are in New Jersey. It is cold, it snows, there are fireplaces. I sat down with Kristen for a long talk. I told her that the real Santa Claus wears a green flight suit and drives an Isuzu pickup truck. His favorite snack is popcorn with Parmesan cheese. I also added she must start getting realistic with her list, Santa doesn't receive his pay until January. Kristen doesn't believe me!

Cathy Ruehl
McGuire OWC Flair, *December 1988*

Our Originals

I remember the Christmas that my husband, Buck, and I gave each other the most original gifts...

We were stationed at KI Sawyer AFB in Michigan, and lived just off base in a little bungalow tucked in the forest with a lake for a backyard. With "orders" pending, I thought of the perfect gift for my husband. I contracted a local artist to capture this setting on canvas and paint a picture of our home. When I picked up the painting, I knew it truly was the right gift. I hung it in the ideal spot on the living room wall and almost convinced myself to give it as an early gift. However, Buck was flying and not due to land until 2:30 a.m.—not an ideal time for art appreciation. So I hid the prized picture in a secret place to await the big day.

At 3:00 a.m., Buck arrived home and awakened me with "Sherry, come in the living room—we've got to talk about something." Thoughts flashed through my head as I struggled to the living room, only half awake. You can imagine my surprise when I saw in MY ideal spot, MY nail without MY picture on it. In its place hung a painting I'd never seen before. Buck had contracted a different artist to paint our home—how "original"!

Sherry Marr

Another Perspective

My wife, Irene, and I had great careers. She was a registered nurse in the emergency room in Buffalo, New York's Children's Hospital. I was a systems analyst at Rich Products, also in Buffalo. We owned a home in Niagara Falls and were raising my two children from a previous marriage.

Irene would often get letters from the military encouraging her to join. I always thought it would be a good idea, but we never had time to explore the possibility. A car accident and time off work provided her with the time to research her options.

She joined the Air Force and moved to Scott Air Force Base in Illinois while I stayed in New York. Visiting her on long weekends became too tough on both of us, so I sold our house, quit my job and the kids and I moved to Scott.

It didn't take me long to get a great job working as a senior systems analyst at Emerson Electric in St. Louis (a 45 minute commute). Things soon got hectic raising two children, nurturing two careers and taking care of home life. It was especially difficult when Irene went to Oman for three months during the Gulf War. But, being a military spouse, I learned to adapt. As one of the few male spouses I would find myself the only guy at support meetings, but everyone made me feel welcome.

Life was great for five years. Then Irene got orders to Ramstein, Germany. The children were ready to go off on their own and we were excited about an adventure in Europe. With my background in computers I figured I could get a job anywhere. Reality struck when we got to Germany and I discovered finding work could sometimes be tough for a military spouse—especially if you have years of experience.

Having worked in the computer industry in very stressful jobs, I was ready to enjoy life anyway, so I volunteered at the USO. That turned into a paid job and soon I was giving orientation tours to new arrivals in Germany.

Before long I had twenty tour guides working for me and I was conducting tours on my own, along with developing new ones. Wow! A tour guide in Europe! One weekend in France, the next in the Netherlands, and the next cruising up the Rhine River, pointing out castles.

But the best part was the military community. Military families really stick together. Even far away from "home" we had a tight-knit community where we looked out for each other. I was proud to be a part of it and did my best to make it better.

The first time Irene came home and said she was thinking of joining the Air Force I had told her I would be with her all the way, even if my career suffered. I also mentioned that I had no desire to go to the Far East. Japan or Korea held no interest for me.

Well, you guessed it. After three years in Germany, Irene came home one day with the good news/bad news. The good news—they offered her a job as the commander of a health and wellness center. The bad news—it was in Yokota, Japan. Oh well, time to pack and off we went, me trying to keep a smile all the way.

It was tough trying to find work in Germany, but Japan was even worse. Yokota is twenty-eight miles from Tokyo in a very densely populated area. Traveling was out. It could take an hour to go twenty miles in bumper-to-bumper traffic. I wasn't too fond of the area, but the base had that wonderful sense of community spirit that I liked. Military communities are like living in Mayberry RFD.

In hopes of getting involved I decided to join the Officers' Spouses' Club. I was the only male at the first meeting I attended. To my surprise I was not made to feel out of place or unwanted. So I signed up to help at the club's Thrift Shop until I could find a "real" job.

It was the first time I had ever been in a thrift shop and this place needed help. The manager had left Japan several months earlier and it showed. After a month of volunteering I was asked to be the manager. It was a paid position—however, the pay was nominal.

My answer was yes, but just until I could find a "real" job. All the shop needed was someone to treat it as a business. Having such experience I took on the challenge. The work was rewarding and provided me with a great opportunity to give back to the Air Force community I enjoyed so much. All profits went to scholarships. It was a reasonable place to shop, and people could sell or donate their good used articles. It seemed to fill a gap in the community because the BX was the only other place to shop. I jokingly refer to our Thrift Shop as the Yokota Wal-Mart substitute.

The year before I took over as manager they gave away $8,500. Since then each year has recorded a significant increase in profits. This next year, which will be my last, we hope to give away $39,000. It is a fun place to shop and a fun place to volunteer. My philosophy is, if you are new to the base, the Thrift Shop is a great place to meet new people; if you have been here for a while, it is a great place to see old friends.

If you are wondering, I actually found a job that would have been a good match for me, but felt I could contribute more to the community at the Thrift Shop. The "real" job meant more money, but it was not what I was looking for.

Besides the Thrift Shop I am involved with our club's semi-annual bazaars. For the last four bazaars I have been the publicity chairman. This seemed a good fit because of the connections I have made advertising for the Thrift Shop.

Being a military spouse, male or female, takes a lot of sacrifice. But like anything else in life, it is how you deal with it. You must make the best of it. Military service is often very tough on its members, so the spouse must be extra supportive. My career may have suffered, but I believe I am a much happier and fulfilled person for it.

Bill Ashker

"At times it's easier to jump out of a plane at 13,000 feet in the middle of the night than to stay at home to raise my daughter, but the rewards are 10 times greater," said Doug Jones, a stay-at-home dad who became an Air Force spouse in 1995. Doug was active-duty Army and a member of the Green Berets prior to trading that in for the ability to stay home full-time with his child after she was born.

Sharon Carney Witter
"Don't Forget Contributions of Military Spouse"
Bolling Beam, May 9, 1997

Homeschooling

"Time to finish up guys! We've got to eat before music lessons and soccer," calls Cheryl Robinson to her four boys. With dad, an Air Force technical sergeant away, it's just another day at home...just another day of being loving mom, on-call chauffeur and full-time teacher—at home.

Training and education are standard components of military life—officer, warrant and enlisted constantly developing their skills. However, another part of the military team spends even more time in this pursuit—the kids.

The Robinsons represent just one of a growing number of military families whose children are part of the 1.5 to 2 million "home schooled" students in America. In most of those homes, mom is the primary teacher. Almost unheard of in the early 1980s, nearly everyone knows of it today. In fact, homeschoolers collectively outnumber the statewide individual public school enrollments of 41 states. As the fastest-growing educational option, parents are turning to home schooling for a range of reasons: safety, academic achievement, philosophy, but stability is one that is especially key among military families.

"Between the moves and Dave's time in the fleet, homeschooling provided one constant...one point of stability for the kids but for all of us too," says Paula Alvarez. She and her two girls have found the sense of continuity through it all has strengthened the family. Although this has meant taking time from her own career, she says, "Nothing I can think of could be more rewarding than being with my girls...They come first."

The first modern homeschooling family in the U.S. Senate has learned the same lesson. "It's…a great experience for all of us. It brought us closer together as a family," explained Karen Santorum, wife of Senator Rick Santorum and mom of two, "and made us a much more important part of our daughter and our son's lives, and we think those were all good things."

Of course, the students have some thoughts too. Many say they enjoy the freedom, the focus, the attention and the depth homeschooling affords them. Some say they miss the ease of interacting with friends while others find more friends coming home every day to join them.

"I like to get up early and try to finish all my book work before the other kids have to get on the school bus," says Elizabeth, age 11. "That way I can do the things I'm most interested in like music, reading, computing."

"It's nice not to have to leave home to do school and it sure does get done faster," says Benjamin, age 13. "I would like to see some more guys during the day (he has four sisters) but that's ok."

"I like my school a lot, says Catherine, age 9. "One of the things I like best is learning how to be a grown up and mom from the real thing—my mom."

"Military life teaches us respect for things whether they are material or verbal," writes one military "brat" online. "You tend to put every effort into a task because you are not sure of how long you will have to do it, versus, 'Oh I'll get around to that, because I know I'm not going anywhere.'"

That's especially true in military family home schools. Parents and kids everywhere are finding the best place to "get it done" with the greatest long-term returns is right where things start—at home.

Brett and Shannon Morris

More or Less

Our family of six arrived in Osan, South Korea, in January of 1987. My "going in" position was that I was one of few spouses who came "command sponsored" and that being the case, I would not expect anything and just be pleased with whatever came my way.

It turned out my resolve was to be tested.

My husband was an A-10 pilot, flying out of Suwon, which was about a thirty-minute drive from Osan. Each family was allowed only one vehicle so I soon learned that I was either going to walk a lot or take taxicabs. I never had the car.

Our new home was in the on-base housing facility called Mustang Valley Village. It is a high-rise apartment complex with our front door on the top floor, up five flights of stairs… thirteen concrete steps per flight. (Guess how I know!)

The commissary was relatively close to the apartment, so I decided I would do my grocery shopping with my two youngest children while my two older ones were away in Seoul at the high school. My girls were three and five at the time.

Like all good military, I stocked up on the first trip. The taxi driver had his hands full getting all my bags in the trunk of the taxi, but he managed. He then drove us to our apartment.

Upon arrival, I noticed he didn't get out of the car, but only popped the trunk lid. I thought I might as well get started unloading while he's doing whatever it is he's doing. (In my mind, he was still going to get out, help me unload the groceries and carry them up the five flights of stairs.) Was I ever in for a rude awakening. Not only was he not going to help me carry them up the stairs, he wasn't going to take them out of the trunk either! So, I had the girls stand on the curb while I unloaded bag after bag onto the cement.

I paid the driver and he left. There I was on the curb with two little girls, fifteen bags of groceries, two cases of soda, a large bag of kitty litter, a big bottle of bleach and a huge box of laundry soap. (Did I mention it was January and COLD outside?) I tried to figure out how I could get all those groceries up the stairs and not leave the girls alone. I knew if I left them at the top, they'd let the dog out and get into who knows what kind of trouble. If I left them at the bottom I was afraid they would go into the street.

So, I divided the trip up the stairs into stages. I left them at the bottom while I ferried all the bags to level three. Then, I had the girls wait for me on level three while I ferried the bags to just outside our apartment door on the fifth floor. I didn't want to open the door to our apartment or take the time to put the groceries inside because I was afraid the dog would get out or that it would take too long. The girls came up with me on the last grocery run up the stairs.

Once I had the groceries all sitting inside my apartment on the counter, I treated myself to half a bag of chocolate chip cookies and a diet coke. I decided I earned that.

In the end, I only did my commissary shopping in bulk like that once. I'd forgotten to take into account that I was living in 950 square feet now and not 3,000 like my stateside house. Once I had all the bags of food in my kitchen, it became evident that there wasn't anywhere close to enough room for all I'd bought.

So, I changed my approach from stocking up to shopping for what I needed several times a week, AND I didn't buy more than I could carry in one trip. Since we were relatively close to the commissary, with my new plan, I could even walk and save the taxi fare for bigger excursions.

The good news is that Korea turned out to be one of our all time favorite assignments. We learned how important friends are and how unimportant the size of your house is. We learned that Americans are very spoiled with conveniences and that most of the world gets along fine without them. We learned that being together as a family is worth the sacrifice (a blessing in disguise). We grew closer to each other and have a life-long cultural experience to incorporate into our own life stories. The Korean people are genuinely happy to have us in their country and are warm, giving people. They have a work ethic to be admired and a loving spirit toward children. We learned to appreciate the differences in our cultures and to better understand why people who speak different languages do more than talk differently.

We were blessed to be able to return to Osan, South Korea ten years after our first tour. This time we lived in a bigger apartment (1,350 square feet!) with two less children. (Isn't it funny how often it works out that way?) We no longer had to climb sixty-five stairs to get to our apartment. It was wonderful to return to a people and culture we'd grown to love, to converse with the Korean people, and to enjoy their friendship and hospitality. Our daughters cried when we left. They loved being in Korea, and not one of us would trade the experiences we had either time.

The Air Force gave us an experience to cherish, and we do!

Sue Rodi

$\mathcal{P}$ride

When the day began I was unaware of the valuable lesson I would learn in a short 24-hour period. The Castle Air Force Base Honor Guard was participating in a drill team competition at Nellis Air Force Base in Nevada. My husband asked if I wanted to go and support them. I agreed and off we went to what I thought would be a couple of hours, a banquet, and home again. It turned out to be so much more.

Practice for the drill teams began at 6:30 a.m. John and I went out early to watch, thinking we would stay just a little while. The heat was building and soon it was 108 degrees. All the teams hung in there, practicing and then competing. Every so often one of our honor guard members would come over and tell us what was going to happen next. As the day wore on we could see the effect of the heat on everyone. So, we went to the commissary, bought drinks for our team and decided to stay to encourage their efforts. A couple young airmen came over to thank us for our support and asked why we were staying in the heat. "If you can do it for the wing," I told them, "then we can do it for you."

The competition ended at 4:30 p.m. All the teams were very impressive, but I could sense there was something special about our team. I could see they were doing very well. The precision, determination, sincerity and commitment showed on every member's face.

That evening, at the awards banquet I had the pleasure of sitting with all these young airmen. I asked one young man why he volunteered to be on the honor guard, since it is an additional duty. "When a member of the military passes away," he told me, "I feel it is the honor guard's job to thank that person for their service to our country." He said, "Doing the very best job at a funeral is a privilege, because it is the final salute of gratitude from our country." I could hardly hold back the tears as he spoke. This was a very young man with such deep feelings. I was so proud of him and all the others.

During the evening another young airman thanked me for my support and asked if he could call me "Mom." He wished his family could have been there to see the competition. I was honored and soon the whole team was calling me Mom.

As the awards ceremony started, the senior staff from each base was introduced. When they introduced Castle AFB, my husband was overlooked. I could hear the airmen at our table talking about how the emcee missed "our chief." My husband said not to worry about it, but one young airman got up, went to the head table, spoke to the emcee and promptly corrected the situation. The entire drill team erupted in cheers when John was introduced. Again, I could hardly hold back the tears. We came to cheer them on, and now they were cheering us.

Castle won that night, and won big, taking eight of ten awards. But for me the evening's significance went beyond the trophies and the accolades. To me it was a defining moment about the Air Force. I always wondered why there were so many competitions. All the car washes, the bake sales and efforts to raise money for the teams seemed like so much work.

That day I realized the value of teamwork. I saw it in action. I saw how each airman had to rely on the other for precision, decision, timing and strength. I saw the faith the leader of the honor guard displayed when he walked through twirling rifles. I saw encouragement and I saw people becoming buddies, putting differences aside. These are elements needed in times of conflict. I learned firsthand the importance of good leaders, senior leaders, believing in and supporting their people and realized just how far that support went toward morale. It all finally made sense to me.

I also saw pride in uniform. I saw respect and dignity. I saw it all and I learned it from the youngest members of our Air Force.

What a difference a day makes.

Danna Shipman

Reflections at Retirement

Timothy,

We've been in the Air Force nearly 24 years and in that time we've had 19 different addresses and about that many cars…most of them used and most, Volkswagen Beetles.

We've lived in trailers, base houses, people's basements, apartments (even one-bedroom units with the bathroom in the hall) and occasionally houses of our own.

We've moved when I was nine months pregnant and due in two weeks; I hand carried my medical records only to have the base hospital say they couldn't take me (not enough doctors and too many pregnant people).

We've spent the weekend I was due self-help painting a three-bedroom base house just so we could have a place to live.

We've survived hurricanes, floods, tornadoes, and earthquakes.

We've suffered through the gut-wrenching agony of losing eleven friends in airplane accidents.

We've been separated due to wars, remotes, TDYs and sitting alert with airplanes.

We've had the opportunity to live in or visit 35 different states and about 10 different countries.

We've stood with the "Bobbie" at 10 Downing Street.

We've climbed to the top of the Eiffel Tower.

We've ridden the canal boats in Venice.

We've skied in Austria and camped in Switzerland.

We've gone to the Tulip Festival in Holland.

We've even attended mass at St. Peter's in Rome.

We've managed, through all of this, to raise two incredibly normal children and keep one faithful marriage alive.

Timothy, it has been one "hell" of a ride; and if given the opportunity to do it over again, I would, and I would definitely do it with you.

Love, Pam

Pam Chatagnier

Contributors

I would like to acknowledge the following individuals, publishers and organizations for permission to reprint the following material. The articles I have written and those in the public domain are not listed.

A Cruise to the Orient by Beverly Bogie. Reprinted with permission of the author.

A Farewell to the "SAC" Wife. Randolph OWC *Windicator,* October 1992. Reprinted with permission of the Randolph Officers' Wives' Club.

...A Memorial Day Wish Comes True by Andrea Tortora. Reprinted with permission of *USA Today.* ©1999.

A Place In My Heart by Cynthia Schramm. Reprinted with permission of the author.

A Toast To Good Friends by Lois Hansen. Reprinted with permission of Army Times.

A Trunkload of Memories by Carolyn Denise Quick Tillery. Reprinted with permission of the author.

Airman's Attic by Jerri Schoeck. Reprinted with permission of the author.

Alphabet Soup by Maryellen Mills. Reprinted with permission of the author.

Another Perspective by Bill Ashker. Reprinted with permission of the author.

Knowledge of Sacrifices Must Be Passed Down by Leslie Smith. Reprinted with permission of the author and with permission of *Army Times*.

Love and Devotion by Sandra Troeber. Reprinted with permission of the author.

Moonlight and Roses by Sandra Troeber. Reprinted with permission of the author.

More or Less by Sue Rodi. Reprinted with permission of the author.

Nancy Harkness Love reprinted courtesy of *The American Experience*, ©WGBH Boston.

No Greater Love by Sandra Troeber. Reprinted with permission of the author.

Off We Go Into the Wild Blue Yonder by Colonel Murray Green, USAF, Ret. Reprinted with permission of the author.

Our Originals by Sherry Marr. Reprinted with permission of the author.

Portable Palettes—Lasting Friendship by Joan Brown. Reprinted with permission of the author. ©Joan Brown.

Precious Moments by Robin Potter. Reprinted with permission of the author.

Pride by Danna Shipman. Reprinted with permission of the author.

Recipe For An Unforgettable Dinner by Carol Garrison. Reprinted with permission of the author.

Reflections at Retirement by Pam Chatagnier. Reprinted with permission of the author.

About the Author

Paulette "PK" Johnson grew up in Illinois. She graduated from the University of Miami where she met her husband Si. For the past 33 years, she has been an Air Force spouse and has shared that lifestyle with many military spouses around the world. Their collective experience is what makes this book possible.

Have a Story to Share?

Do you have a memory, story, anecdote or poem about life as an Air Force spouse? If you would like to share it with others in a future volume of *Wings Of Our Own,* please send it to me.

P. K. Johnson
308 Skyhill Road
Alexandria, VA 22314
E-mail: wingsofourown@aol.com

Would You Like More Copies?

▼ Visit the Wings website at
www.wingsofourown.com
▼ E-mail order to wingsofourown@aol.com
▼ Send your request to:
P. K. Johnson
308 Skyhill Road
Alexandria, VA 22314

Include your name, address and telephone number on all correspondence.